Getting Away from it All!

Have you ever had an expensive holiday? Where did you go? What did you do?

1 Discussion Words

Check any new words and mark the strong stress in each word or phrase:

Chief Executive   Mauritius   stepdaughter
Stuart   getaway   to jet off   supplier   PA
manufacturing firm   sandcastles   karaoke   wi-fi
sunbathing   resort   reports   tropical island
sales forecasts   quarter   Melanie   factory

2 Dialogue

Read the following dialogue aloud with your partner:

1 Stuart Willis is the Chief Executive of a small manufacturing firm based in Halifax, West Yorkshire. He recently jetted off to Mauritius for a romantic getaway at a luxury resort, with his second wife Denise and their stepdaughter Chloe. However, despite the sun, sand, and karaoke competitions, he just can't seem to relax. He phones his PA in England for a chat:

5 **Melanie:** So how's your holiday going? Are you having a lovely time? What are you doing right now?

Stuart: Well, Denise is sunbathing and Chloe is making sandcastles on the beach, but I'm going through some sales forecasts for next quarter…

Melanie: Oh, I thought you were going on holiday to get away from it all. You should be sunning yourself. **Treat yourself!** It's the **holiday of a lifetime**.

10 **Stuart:** What's Tom doing today? Is he driving to Leeds to meet that supplier?

Melanie: Yes, he's meeting them at one o'clock for lunch.

Stuart: And are the lads in the factory **getting on alright**?

Melanie: Yes, I think so. They're hoping to finish two orders by five o'clock. Are you **checking up on us**?

Stuart: You know what they say, Melanie – **while the cat's away, the mice will play**.

15 **Melanie:** Well, **everybody's working flat out** to meet the targets you set us before you left. Don't worry – your deputy is taking care of everything.

Stuart: Good, good! Well, I can't chat any longer. I have to hurry. **Time is money**, you know!

Melanie: **What on earth** are you hurrying for? You're on a tropical island in the middle of the Indian Ocean!

Stuart: You know I'm a bit of a **control freak**. That's why I'm finishing off these two reports and then later 20 we're going back to the resort.

Melanie: Oh, right. So you're not a total **workaholic**. You will have a chance to unwind with your family?

Stuart: Well, we're going so I can email some new reports to you. I can't get wi-fi on the beach!

3 New English Alphabet and Connected Speech

Can you find this sentence in the text? Practise saying it aloud:

uh y Ha ving uh Lu vlii Taim?
 a b   c   d   e   f   g   h

1. There are ____ syllables in this sentence.
2. The stressed syllables are _____.
3. The stressed vowel sounds are _____.
4. There are ____ Schwa sounds on _____.

5. There's an embedded Schwa sound on ____.
6. uh represents two different words: ____ and ____.
7. There are ____ friendly consonant sounds on…
8. There are ____ weak-stressed syllables.

4 Sentence Blocks – Present Continuous

*Underline examples of **present continuous** form in the text, then practise the sentence blocks.*

What time does present continuous indicate in each sentence?

1. Chloe is making sandcastles on the beach.   *who / what / where*

2. He's meeting them at one o'clock for lunch.   *when / what / why / who*

3. They're hoping to finish two orders by five o'clock.   *what (x2) / when / who*

While the cat's away, the mice will play!

5 Non-Literal English – Idioms, Phrasal Verbs, and Slang

Look at the idioms which are highlighted in the text (left).
Match each one to a phrase below:

a) working without problems
b) spying on somebody
c) working very hard
d) if you waste time you waste cash
e) do something that you enjoy
f) people won't work hard if the boss is absent
g) a person who lives to work
h) a trip you can only afford once
i) why??
j) somebody who must be in charge

Title

"To get away from it all" is an idiom meaning to have a relaxing break – a time when you can forget about work and problems.

Lead-in – Discussion Questions

Extensions: Prepare further discussion questions on this lesson topic – the tension between work and holidays. Or get SS to write their own and ask each other, perhaps changing partners a few times during the activity.

Pictures

Extensions: SS describe the pictures and how they are related to the lesson. SS look for other relevant pictures on the internet.

1 Discussion Words

The stressed syllable(s) are underlined:

Chief Ex<u>ec</u>utive   Mau<u>ri</u>tius   <u>step</u>daughter   <u>Stu</u>art   <u>get</u>away   to jet <u>off</u>   sup<u>plier</u>   <u>P</u> <u>A</u>   manu<u>fac</u>turing firm

<u>san</u>dcastles   kara<u>o</u>ke   <u>wi-fi</u>   <u>sun</u>bathing   re<u>sort</u>   re<u>ports</u>   tropical <u>is</u>land   <u>sales</u> forecasts   <u>quar</u>ter

<u>Mel</u>anie   <u>fac</u>tory

Extensions: Use the Discussion Word Questions from Talk a Lot Elementary Books 1-3 or Talk a Lot Intermediate Book 1, or use the Big Word Game or Talk a Lot Bingo from Talk a Lot Elementary Handbook.

2 Dialogue

Extensions: 1. SS improvise role plays based on the situation, e.g. what happened before or after? What happened back at the hotel? Imagine the other characters: Denise, Chloe, the lads at the factory, etc. 2. SS choose one character from the text and devise and perform a monologue as that character. They could practise different verb forms by setting the monologue before the time of the action (using future verb forms), during the action (using present verb forms), or after the action (using past verb forms).

3 New English Alphabet and Connected Speech

The sentence is from line 5: "Are you having a lovely time?"

1. There are **8** syllables in this sentence.
2. The stressed syllables are **Ha , Lu , and Taim [c, f, and h]**.
3. The stressed vowel sounds are **a , u , and ai**.
4. There are **3** Schwa sounds on **a, b, and e**.
5. There's an embedded Schwa sound on **b**.
6. uh represents two different words: **Are** and **a**.
7. There are **2** friendly consonant sounds on **d [ng] and h [m]**.
8. There are **5** weak-stressed syllables. [a, b, d, e, and g.]

Extensions: Translate other sentences from the text into the NEA and answer the same questions about them. Look at sentence stress and connected speech features. How do the syllables connect together? See Talk a Lot Foundation Course for more ideas.

4 Sentence Blocks – Present Continuous

There are many examples of present continuous form in the text, for example:

5   So how**'s** your holiday **going**? **Are** you **having** a lovely time? What **are** you **doing** right now?

6   Well, Denise **is sunbathing** and Chloe **is making** sandcastles on the beach.

etc.

Note: parts of the text *in italics* will vary. SS should use their own ideas:

1. Chloe is making sandcastles on the beach.

In this sentence present continuous indicates: **now / at the moment**.

Who is making sandcastles on the beach? / Chloe is. / Is Chloe making sandcastles on the beach? / Yes, she is. / Is *Bob* making sandcastles on the beach? / No, *he* isn't. *Bob* isn't making sandcastles on the beach. / So…

What is Chloe doing on the beach? / Making sandcastles. / Is Chloe making sandcastles on the beach? / Yes, she is. / Is Chloe *reading a book* on the beach? / No, she isn't. Chloe isn't *reading a book* on the beach. / So…

Where is Chloe making sandcastles? / On the beach. / Is Chloe making sandcastles on the beach? / Yes, she is. / Is Chloe making sandcastles *in the park*? / No, she isn't. Chloe isn't making sandcastles *in the park*. / So…

2. He's meeting them at one o'clock for lunch.

In this sentence present continuous indicates: **future**.

When is he meeting them for lunch? / At one o'clock. / Is he meeting them at one o'clock for lunch? / Yes, he is. / Is he meeting them at *two o'clock* for lunch? / No, he isn't. He isn't meeting them at *two o'clock* for lunch. / So…

What is he doing at one o'clock? / Meeting them for lunch. / Is he meeting them at one o'clock for lunch? / Yes, he is. / Is he *playing golf* with them at one o'clock? / No, he isn't. He isn't *playing golf* with them at one o'clock. / So…

Why is he meeting them at one o'clock? / For lunch. / Is he meeting them at one o'clock for lunch? / Yes, he is. / Is he meeting them at one o'clock *for dinner*? / No, he isn't. He isn't meeting them at one o'clock *for dinner*. / So…

Who is he meeting at one o'clock for lunch? / Them (that supplier). / Is he meeting them at o'clock for lunch? / Yes, he is. / Is he meeting *his dentist* at one o'clock for lunch? / No, he isn't. He isn't meeting *his dentist* at one o'clock for lunch. / So…

3. They're hoping to finish two orders by five o'clock.

In this sentence present continuous indicates: **now / at the moment**.

What are they hoping to finish by five o'clock? / Two orders. / Are they hoping to finish two orders by five o'clock? / Yes, they are. / Are they hoping to finish *four orders* by five o'clock? / No, they aren't. They aren't hoping to finish *four orders* by five o'clock. / So…

What are they hoping to do by five o'clock? / Finish two orders. / Are they hoping to finish two orders by five o'clock? / Yes, they are. / Are they hoping to finish *four orders* by five o'clock? / No, they aren't. They aren't hoping to finish *four orders* by five o'clock. / So…

When are they hoping to finish two orders by? / (By) five o'clock. / Are they hoping to finish two orders by five o'clock? / Yes, they are. / Are they hoping to finish two orders by *three o'clock*? / No, they aren't. They aren't hoping to finish two orders by *three o'clock*. / So…

Who are hoping to finish two orders by five o'clock? / They (the lads) are. / Are they hoping to finish two orders by five o'clock? / Yes, they are. / Are *your parents* hoping to finish two orders by five o'clock? / No, they aren't. *My parents* aren't hoping to finish two orders by five o'clock. / So…

Extensions: Use other sentences from the text (or sentences written by SS on the same topic) and practise building sentence blocks using a variety of question words. SS work individually, in pairs, in small groups, or as a whole class. Or SS could focus on the verb form in question – present continuous – to create more starting sentences and sentence blocks. See Talk a Lot Elementary Handbook for further ideas.

5 Non-Literal English – Idioms, Phrasal Verbs, and Slang

Treat yourself!	e) do something that you enjoy
holiday of a lifetime	h) a trip you can only afford once
getting on alright	a) working without problems
checking up on us	b) spying on somebody
while the cat's away, the mice will play	f) people won't work hard if the boss is absent
everybody's working flat out	c) working very hard
Time is money	d) if you waste time you waste cash
What on earth	i) why??
control freak	j) somebody who must be in charge
workaholic	g) a person who lives to work

Extensions: 1. SS could translate the non-literal phrases into literal ones, and practise the dialogue again so that it is entirely literal – wholly grey language – instead of having the colour that the idioms, phrasal verbs, and slang bring. 2. Find other idioms, phrasal verbs, and/or slang on the same topic of work and holidays.

The aim of any Talk a Lot course is for students to practise and improve their speaking, listening, and pronunciation skills. Along the way the student will learn plenty of new vocabulary – including non-literal English expressions, such as idioms, phrasal verbs, and slang – and also practise reading, writing, and grammar skills, e.g. verb forms, word order, parts of a sentence, and so on.

This two-page spread provides an organised sequence of learning activities for students at intermediate level (CEF B2). We believe that there is easily enough material here for a 90-minute lesson. Of course, how long the material lasts will depend on a variety of factors, such as the level of your students, and how familiar they are with Talk a Lot techniques. If you used some or all of the extension activities, you could make the material last much longer.

Although many of the activities in this book can be used without having previously studied with Talk a Lot material, e.g. the reading comprehension tests, this is the second Talk a Lot Intermediate course book and the author has assumed that students will have some prior knowledge of Talk a Lot methodology, e.g. knowing how to make sentence blocks, and how to find the stressed syllables and sounds in a word or phrase; or how to read the New English Alphabet.

WORK GETTING YOU DOWN?

1 Non-Literal English – Phrasal Verbs

Check the meaning of any new phrasal verbs. Use them to complete the gaps in the text below. Change forms where necessary.

get away with sth   **fight off** sth

get sby **down**   **get by**   **throw up**

get sth **out of** sth   **come up with** sth

play up   **come on**   **crack on with** sth

TIP: sth = something   sby = somebody

2 Discussion

a) Read about four different employees who are having problems at work:

Tom, 28, from Luton: I'm so busy at work normally that I never have enough time to do all my housework, and now my partner's nagging me to a) _____ a spot of decorating. She's bought the paint and rollers and she's told me I'll have to take a few days off work. I can't think I'll be able to b) _____ a good enough excuse – or even if I'll c) _____ – but I don't know who I'm more scared of upsetting – my boss or my girlfriend…

Gloria, 34, from Stirling: Last week I rang in sick and pretended I'd been d) _____ all night, and was suffering from a bad case of diarrhoea. I laid it on thick and I could tell the guy who answered the phone didn't want to hear all the details… I usually tell them that my back's been e) _____. The real problem is that I'm being bullied at work by one of my colleagues, but I can't discuss it with my line manager, because he's one of her best friends…

Suzy, 23, from Nottingham (above): I fell out with a woman at work – well, now we're former friends, I suppose. I said something I shouldn't have done and things just got out of hand. You know, other people found out and they, well, most of them anyway, ended up taking her side, and I've been persona non grata ever since.

So I phoned in sick on Monday and told them I'm f) _____ an infection, which g) _____ suddenly. I've been at home all week, too frightened to go back to work. It's really h) _____, because it feels like they've all got it in for me…

Frank, 36, from Swindon: I enjoy my job, although I feel that I should be getting paid more, because I've been there for more than ten years. Recently I was told that I wouldn't be getting a pay rise this year, and the staff Christmas party has been cancelled due to lack of funds. Would you believe it!

I sometimes think about quitting and getting a new job, 'cause I don't i) _____, but all of my friends, you know, are there and I can't be bothered – to be honest – to look for anything different. I guess I'll just have to keep pulling sickies, but I don't really like doing it 'cause I know it's wrong. So… I'm sure they can j) _____ without me though.

b) Discuss with your partner: what would you do in each situation?

QUICK FACT > THE AVERAGE WORKER IN THE UK HAS 7 DAYS OFF SICK FROM WORK EACH YEAR

QUICK FACT > THE MOST COMMON CAUSE OF SICK LEAVE IN THE UK IS STRESS

(Have you ever been off work due to stress?)

3 Discussion

Look at the reasons that people sometimes give for being off work sick. Imagine that you are an employer, and say whether you would consider them to be valid excuses or not – and why:

stomach bug

I hate my job

I'm being bullied at work

food poisoning

sickness and diarrhoea

I've just split up with my partner

I'm caring for a sick relative

flu symptoms

taking the car to the garage

splitting headache

appointment at the dentist's

RSI (repetitive strain injury)

I'm a lone parent and I need to sort out something

I've got a migraine

problems with childcare

crippling back pain

going to a job interview

stress

I've earned a long weekend

4 Discussion Words

*Look at the words and phrases in pink type. Find the **strong-stressed syllable** in each one and circle all of the **Schwa sounds**.*

Sometimes I just fancy a duvet day!

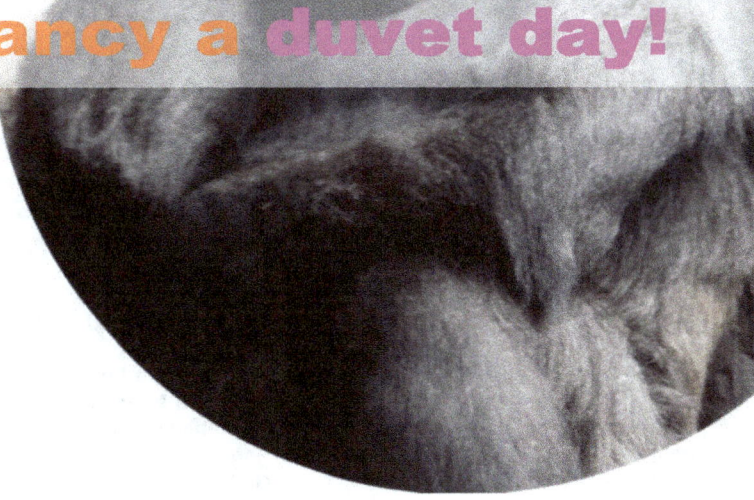

5 Pronunciation – Sound Connections

*Look at four phrases from the text (in blue). What are the **sound connections** between them? Should we use **intrusion** or **elision**? Explain why, then practise saying them:*

  a) She's **bought the** paint and rollers…
  b) **Recently I** was told…
  c) the guy **who answered** the phone…
  d) So I phoned in sick on Monday and **told them**…

6 Role Plays

Work with your partner to create a short role play or dialogue based on each situation in the text. You could imagine each one from the point of view of different characters, e.g. the employee, their boss, their partner, their colleagues, and so on. You could also show what happens next in the situation, or the events that led up to it…

7 Sentence Blocks – Present Perfect Passive

Practise the sentence blocks. What time does present perfect passive indicate? Why is passive voice used here?

The staff Christmas party has been cancelled due to lack of funds.

what (x2) / why / which

Title

"Work getting you down?" is a short question form of the phrasal verb "to get sby down" (see below). It literally means: "Is work making you feel unhappy at the moment?"

Pictures

Extensions: SS describe the pictures and how they are related to the lesson. SS look for other relevant pictures on the internet.

1 Non-Literal English – Phrasal Verbs

Phrasal Verb:	Literal Meaning:	Gap:	Form in the Text:
get away with sth	be not caught doing something wrong	c)	get away with it
fight off sth	recover from sth, e.g. an illness or infection	f)	fighting off
get sby down	make somebody feel upset or depressed	h)	getting me down
get by	manage / handle sth / cope	j)	get by
throw up	vomit / be sick	d)	throwing up
get sth out of sth	benefit or profit from doing sth	i)	get anything out of it
come up with sth	think up / invent	b)	come up with
play up	cause discomfort or pain	e)	playing up
come on	start	g)	came on
crack on with sth	a colloquial form of "get on with sth", meaning to continue working on a project after a break	a)	crack on with

Extensions: See Talk a Lot Intermediate Book 1 for more interesting ways to practise phrasal verbs.

2 Discussion

b) Answers will vary. Encourage SS to look up any new words and expressions.

Extensions: SS could write a formal email or letter to their manager explaining how they feel about their job, and what they would like to change about it.

3 Discussion

Answers will vary. Encourage SS to look up any new words and expressions.

Extensions: The pair or small group discussion could lead into a wider class debate, with SS putting their views on both sides of the argument, e.g. a zero-tolerance (strict) approach to staff absence versus a more "softly-softly" (lenient) approach. For example, if an employer comes down very hard on somebody who has taken a duvet day, it could be counter-productive in that the employee might start actively looking for another job. But if the employer is too lenient, however, it could lead to further working days being lost due to unnecessary sick leave. SS could research and debate the different points of view.

4 Discussion Words

The strong-stressed syllable(s) are underlined. Schwa sounds are indicated in grey type:

stomach bug
bullied
food poisoning
sickness
diarrhoea
split up
relative

flu symptoms
splitting headache
appointment
RSI
repetitive strain injury
lone parent

migraine
childcare
back pain
job interview
stress
long weekend
duvet day

Extensions: Use the Discussion Word Questions from Talk a Lot Elementary Books 1-3 or Talk a Lot Intermediate Book 1, or use the Big Word Game or Talk a Lot Bingo from Talk a Lot Elementary Handbook. You might decide to focus on the topic of sound connections, which is practised in the next exercise. You can find out more about this topic in Talk a Lot Foundation Course. You could also get SS to put each word or phrase into their own sentence, using a verb form of their (or your) choice.

5 Pronunciation – Sound Connections

Phrase:	Sound Connection:	We Should Use:	NEA (Phonetic) Translation:
a) bought the	cc	elision	Bor_ th

Why? We remove the t at the end of "bought" to make it easier to say the two consonant sounds together. We should also use a glottal stop to make the transition sound more natural.

b) Recently I	vv	intrusion	Ree sn_ lii yai

Why? When two vowel sounds meet, we need to add a consonant sound – w, y, or r. In this case, the y sound occurs naturally between "Recently" and "I".

c) who answered	vv	intrusion	hoo Warn sd

Why? As in b), above, we need to add a consonant sound, in this case the w sound occurs naturally between "who" and "answered".

d) told them	cc	elision	Teul_ thm

Why? We remove the d at the end of "told" to make it easier to say the two consonant sounds together. We should also use a glottal stop to make the transition sound more natural.

Extensions: SS look at sound connections between phrases taken from the text, or from the discussion words, above, or any phrases that they can find or invent. In this exercise we focus on two features of connected speech – intrusion and elision – but you could extend the exercise to include any or all of the other features, i.e. glottal stop, linking, assimilation, contraction, and r-linking. SS could write each phrase using the NEA (as above) to show which sounds are used and which are missing or have been added.

6 Role Plays

Answers will vary. Why not have a class competition to see which pair or group can come up with the best short drama?

Extensions: See Talk a Lot Elementary Handbook for more ideas and guidance on developing role plays. One tip is to start to add more detail to the scene. SS could invent more information about each character, e.g. in the first short text we know that Tom is from Luton and has a partner, but do they have any children? Do they *want* to have children? Are they planning to get married? Have they just moved into their house? Is that why his partner wants him to hurry up and do the decorating? What's her name? Are they happy together? SS work together to add layers of detail which make the role play much richer. Of course, there are no right or wrong answers here: the idea is for SS to use their imaginations and to create something that can be assessed by the teacher in terms of spoken English, pronunciation, use of English, vocabulary, and so on.

7 Sentence Blocks – Present Perfect Passive

Note: parts of the text *in italics* will vary. SS should use their own ideas:

The staff Christmas party has been cancelled due to lack of funds.

In this sentence present perfect passive indicates: **recent past**, e.g. in the last 24 hours. The use of passive voice indicates that either we don't know who cancelled it, or that this information is so well-known that it is not worth mentioning it – i.e. the manager, or the board of directors, etc.

What has been cancelled due to lack of funds? / The staff Christmas party. / Has the staff Christmas party been cancelled due to lack of funds? / Yes, it has. / Has the *children's carol concert* been cancelled due to lack of funds? / No, it hasn't. The *children's carol concert* hasn't been cancelled due to lack of funds. / So…

What has happened? / The staff Christmas party has been cancelled due to lack of funds. / Has the staff Christmas party been cancelled due to lack of funds? / Yes, it has. / Has *the deputy manager dressed up as Santa Claus*? / No, *she* hasn't. *The deputy manager* hasn't *dressed up as Santa Claus.* / So…

Why has the staff Christmas party been cancelled? / Due to lack of funds. / Has the staff Christmas party been cancelled due to lack of funds? / Yes, it has. / Has the staff Christmas party been cancelled due to *lack of interest*? / No, it hasn't. The staff Christmas party hasn't been cancelled due to *lack of interest.* / So…

Which party has been cancelled due to lack of funds? / The staff Christmas party. / Has the staff Christmas party been cancelled due to lack of funds? / Yes, it has. / Has the *children's party* been cancelled due to lack of funds? / No, it hasn't. The *children's party* hasn't been cancelled due to lack of funds. / So...

blocks using a variety of question words. SS work individually, in pairs, in small groups, or as a whole class. Or SS could focus on the verb form in question – present perfect passive – to create more starting sentences and sentence blocks. See Talk a Lot Elementary Handbook for further ideas.

About **Talk a Lot Intermediate Book 2**

The aim of any Talk a Lot course is for students to practise and improve their speaking, listening, and pronunciation skills. Along the way the student will learn plenty of new vocabulary – including non-literal English expressions, such as idioms, phrasal verbs, and slang – and also practise reading, writing, and grammar skills, e.g. verb forms, word order, parts of a sentence, and so on.

This two-page spread provides an organised sequence of learning activities for students at intermediate level (CEF B2). We believe that there is easily enough material here for a 90-minute lesson. Of course, how long the material lasts will depend on a variety of factors, such as the level of your students, and how familiar they are with Talk a Lot techniques. If you used some or all of the extension activities, you could make the material last much longer.

al, e.g. the reading comprehension tests, this is the second Talk a Lot Intermediate course book and the author has assumed that students will have some prior knowledge of Talk a Lot methodology, e.g. knowing how to make sentence blocks, and how to find the stressed syllables and sounds in a word or phrase; or how to read the New English Alphabet.

The Work

1 Dialogue – Part 1

Read the dialogue aloud with your partner. Check any new words or expressions in your dictionary:

The annual Work Fun Day is approaching at Teknekat, a multinational based in Bristol. Employees from the company's five main sites are going to come together at Head Office to raise money for charity. Two employees discuss the forthcoming event:

Keisha: It's the Work Fun Day tomorrow. Are you gonna do anything?
Jack: Apart from come into work as usual? No.
Keisha: Why not? It should be really fun, I reckon. I'm getting people to sponsor me to give up chocolate for the day – a complete chocolate ban.
Jack: [Sarcastically] Well, that should be easy for you.
Keisha: Why?
Jack: I was being sarcastic.
Keisha: Oh. Are you gonna wear your own clothes tomorrow?
Jack: Of course. I wear my own clothes every day. Whose else would I wear?
Keisha: No. I mean you have to pay a pound and you don't have to wear a suit.
Jack: [Sarcastically] Well, that'll be great, won't it? It's a **safe bet** I'll be in my normal office clothes.
Keisha: Oh, don't be a party pooper! What? You're not going to join in the fun?
Jack: I don't know. It's a definite maybe. Let's just leave it at that.
Keisha: Oh, go on, Jack! It'll be a laugh!
Jack: Well it's a bit of an oxymoron, isn't it? Work Fun Day. I don't come here to have fun. I come to work to get paid – and that's all.

2 Discussion Words & Pronunciation Focus

Look at the list of typical company departments (in red type below).
a) Check any new words or phrases and mark the stressed syllables
b) Underline the **suffixes**, e.g. Manage*ment*. Remember that in English pronunciation, suffixes are not usually stressed. This helps us when we're looking for the stressed syllable in a word, because we can usually discount the suffix

Sarcasm!

We use sarcasm when we say something that clearly isn't true, with the intention of emphasising the truth and criticising or mocking somebody or something. In this text Jack is being sarcastic because he doesn't like the idea of a work fun day. He says the opposite of what he means, but Keisha knows his true meaning, e.g. he says **"Well, that'll be great, won't it?"** but both know that he means it won't be.

3 Information Exchange

Work with a partner. Decide who is A and B. If you are A, use the grid below, if B use the other grid. Ask questions and complete the missing info in columns 1 and 2. Don't read the other page – find out the information by listening!

Department	1 Main Responsibilities	2 Funds Raised (8am - 1pm)	3 Funds Raised (1 - 4pm)	4 Funds Raised (Dept. Total)
Management	planning the way forward; troubleshooting			£597.38
Human Resources (HR)		£228.10		
Finance	payroll; doing the accounts			£170.75
Legal	dealing with legal issues; giving legal advice		£156.79	
Sales		£580.23		
Marketing	making sure customers know about the products	£779.12		
Production		£668.43		£1,090.87
Distribution			£234.68	
Information Technology (IT)	providing and maintaining computer equipment and software		£108.61	
Research and Development (R&D)			£216.88	
Customer Service	ensuring the customer is happy and will order again	£640.53		£880.55
Maintenance		£833.86		
			Total Raised:	

a) Which department has raised the most before lunch? Give possible reasons.
b) Have you ever taken part in a work fun day? What was it like? How much money did you raise?

– and other oxymorons

4 Dialogue – Part 2

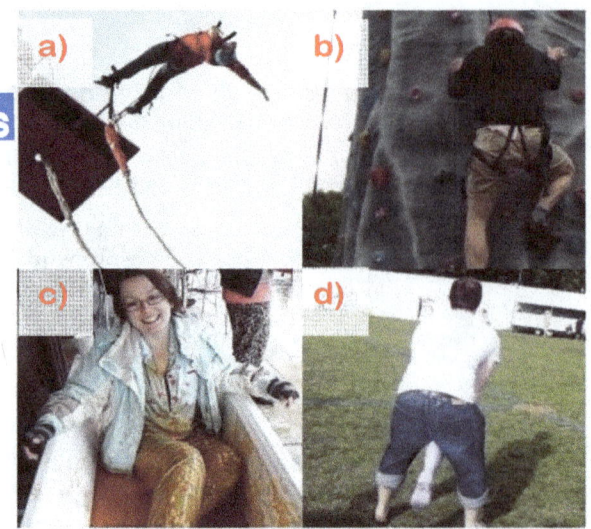

Friday, 9.45am – the staff car park has been transformed into a maze of different fundraising activities:

Keisha: Hi, Jack! So you *did* wear your own clothes after all.
Jack: You know, it's the same difference to me. I mean, it's an open secret that I'm the best-dressed guy in HR, so I thought I'd better make an effort and dress up for the big day.
Keisha: [Sarcastically] Ha ha! Seriously funny, Jack. Hey – did you see the guys from Maintenance doing that bungee jump? Amazing! I thought it was all gonna end in tears. Could've been **pretty ugly**.
Jack: How's your sponsored chocolate ban going?
Keisha: Actually, it's been a bit of a minor disaster, really. I've had three Kit Kats already since I got here. And the Sales Department are selling some really delicious-smelling cookies…
Jack: [Sarcastically] Huh! My faith in your willpower has been completely destroyed! I guess I won't need to donate to you then.
Keisha: Well, you can make a contribution – as long as it's cocoa-based!
Jack: Come on, let's go. This is boring.
Keisha: No, Jack, we can't go. We're not allowed. We'll get into trouble.
Jack: [Sarcastically] Oh, I'm really scared.
Keisha: And anyway, my mate's gonna get chucked in a bath of baked beans in a minute.
Jack: [Sarcastically] I can hardly wait!

People in the UK are generally keen to get involved in raising money for charity by doing, sometimes, really strange things! Match each fundraising activity to a picture above:
1. welly wanging   2. sitting in a bath of baked beans
3. bungee jumping   4. climbing wall

5 Non-Literal English – Oxymorons

An oxymoron is a phrase in which the words contradict each other, e.g. **Work Fun Day** is an oxymoron because "work" and "fun" are usually opposite concepts. There are lots of other oxymorons in the dialogues, including, **safe bet** and **pretty ugly**. See if you can find **8 more**, then discuss them with your partner, and try to think of a few more. Do you have oxymorons in your language? If so, give examples.

6 Listening – Track 1.3a

The Fun Day has nearly finished, and it's time for **Bernard Good**, CEO of Teknekat, to announce the total amount raised by each department during the afternoon session. Listen and complete the missing information in columns 3 and 4 of your information exchange grid.

a) Which department has raised the most?
b) How much has the company raised in total?

7 Dialogue – Part 3

Friday, 5.10pm – going home:

Keisha: So – did you enjoy the fun day?
Jack: [Sarcastically] Yes, it's been one of the most incredible days of my life. [Laughing] The best bit was when the scoreboard broke down at the end.
Keisha: Oh, trust you to think that was the best part! You must have enjoyed *something* today. What about the welly wanging competition?
Jack: The truth is that at this kind of event I feel like a social outcast.
Keisha: Why?
Jack: Because I just don't see how you can have fun at work.
Keisha: I'm not even going to answer that. I'll just leave an eloquent silence.
Jack: It's always nice to talk to you. You almost always seem to understand me.
Keisha: Now – are you being sarcastic or not? It's so hard to tell with you.
Jack: Let's discuss it further over a drink. I'll buy you a hot chocolate.
Keisha: Oh, no thanks. I mean, yes, I'll have a drink with you – but no more chocolate. I've eaten enough today to last me till next year's fun day!

3 Information Exchange

Student B's Grid:

	1	**2**	**3**	**4**
Department	**Main Responsibilities**	**Funds Raised (8am - 1pm)**	**Funds Raised (1 - 4pm)**	**Funds Raised (Dept. Total)**
Management		£467.13		£597.38
Human Resources (HR)	finding new staff; caring for employees' needs; training			
Finance		£104.35		£170.75
Legal		£249.79	£156.79	
Sales	selling the products			
Marketing				
Production	manufacturing the products			£1,090.87
Distribution	getting the products in front of customers	£454.56	£234.68	
Information Technology (IT)		£547.90	£108.61	
Research and Development (R&D)	coming up with new products	£487.19	£216.88	
Customer Service				£880.55
Maintenance	taking care of equipment, property, and vehicles			
			Total Raised:	

6 Listening – Track 1.3a

Transcript:

Note: fundraising activities are underlined. Unfamiliar idiomatic expressions are shown in blue type, with literal translations below:

The Fun Day has nearly finished, and it's time for **Bernard Good**, *CEO of Teknekat, to announce the total amount raised by each department during the afternoon session. Listen and complete the missing information in columns 3 and 4 of your information exchange grid.*

Bernard Good:

Well, let me just say a big thank you[1] to everybody who took part in today's work fun day! We all think – I mean, the company directors and I – want to congratulate you. You've all done an absolutely incredible job here today raising funds for Colon Research, our chosen charity for this year's Fun Day. Er, so, without any further ado[2], let me just, er… on to the final scores! As we know, the Maintenance department were leading at lunch, with a total of £833.86 raised – thanks largely, no doubt, to the whole team of mechanics who bravely agreed to do a group bungee jump from the very top[3] of the building.

But I digress… Er, which brings me on to the total funds raised by each department after lunch, between one o'clock and four o'clock. Well, in reverse order, the Finance department, I'm sad to say, raised the least, with just £66.40. But on the other hand I'm pleased to see they were able to discourage employees from spending money, which is one of their functions, so… good. Keep up the good work![4] Er, next were the HR girls – and, er, guys – who raised £102.47, giving their department a grand total of, er, well you can see the department totals there on the old, er, electronic scoreboard. OK, well, the boffins[5] from IT managed to raise £108.61 after lunch, while the Management Team, led by, ahem, yours truly[6], could have done better, I suppose, with £130.25. The Legal team raised, well you can see how they got on there on the scoreboard – and the Distribution bods[7] have also done a really splendid job[8] raising £234.68, although was it absolutely necessary for *fifteen* different members of that team to try and jump in the bath of baked beans? No, I didn't think so.

The Customer Services team have done themselves proud[9] this afternoon, raising £240.02. And a word about R&D too. They did a grand job, considering they are such a small team – and one of them had to pop off[10] to the library after lunch to return some books. So, well done that R&D team! Now, the Sales team raised £196.18, but an hour ago an anonymous donor (it was Tony from HR, in actual fact), handed me an envelope containing a crisp fifty pound note[11]. He wants it to go towards supporting the efforts of the Sales team – who, in my opinion, have done a really great job with the welly wanging competition. And a special mention to Brian, who endured a beard of bees for twelve minutes. Well done, Brian – and get well soon.

So, on to the big-hitters[12]. The departments who've raised the most. Now, the Production department have worked really hard on the abseiling activity and the climbing wall, and don't forget that they also organised the Wear Your Own Clothes to Work scheme, the proceeds of which were included in their total for this morning. They raised an additional £422.44 this afternoon. So… fantastic! A big round of applause, please![13] Er, thank you for your hard work. So, two departments to go. At lunch, Maintenance were on top, but Marketing were nipping at their heels[14]. Well, I'm pleased to be able to announce that… er, wait a moment. Er, something's gone wrong with the old, er, scoreboard. Is anyone from Maintenance around to have a look at it? Well, anyway – your department raised an extra £427.90, and Marketing have an afternoon total of £482.97. So, which department raised the most? Can anybody work it out? And what is the grand total[15] for the whole company?

---

[1] thank you very much; many thanks
[2] without any further hesitation
[3] the top of the building – "very" emphasises "top", indicating that it was a tall building
[4] continue to work hard
[5] clever people; people who are good at working with technology
[6] me
[7] people; folks; team
[8] a very good job
[9] done very well; they can feel proud of their achievement
[10] to go quickly; to run
[11] a new bank note; "crisp" indicates that it is flat and has never been folded
[12] the teams who have done the best; the top contenders
[13] please clap enthusiastically
[14] just behind them in the competition; catching them up
[15] the final score; the total when all of the department totals have been added together

Test Your Vocabulary Skills

100 Great English Oxymorons –
Phrases that Contradict Themselves!

absolutely unsure
accurate estimate
active retirement
act naturally
advanced beginner
all alone
almost always
awfully nice
bad health
bad luck
boxing ring
calculated risk
civil disobedience
civil war
classic rock & roll
clean toilet
clear as mud
cold sweat
common courtesy
completely destroyed
conservative liberal
consistently inconsistent
controlled chaos
criminal justice
crisis management
critical acclaim
deafening silence
definite maybe
eloquent silence
essential luxury
fatally injured
foreign national
free credit
friendly fire
genuine imitation
graduate student
great depression
group of individuals
half full
home office
homework
humanitarian invasion
ill health
incomplete cure
incredibly dull
initial conclusion
intense apathy
last initial
limited freedom
liquid gas

lower inflation
minor disaster
minor miracle
modern history
never again
new tradition
non-alcoholic beer
non-working mother
nothing much
numbing sensation
open secret
one hundred and ten percent
one size fits all
only choice
organized chaos
original copy
partially completed
passive aggressive
peacekeeping force
perfectly normal
permanent substitute
personal computer
practice test
pretty ugly
pure 100% orange juice from concentrate
real polyester
recent history
relative stranger
required donation
resident alien
retired worker
safe bet
safety hazard
same difference
school holiday
science fiction
second best
seriously funny
short distance
single copy
social outcast
student teacher
think out loud
toll free
tough love
unbiased opinion
unfunny joke
virtual reality
working party
young adult

Title

"The Work Fun Day – and Other Oxymorons". In the UK it is traditional for company employees to get involved with fundraising activities on certain days of the year, to support causes such as the BBC's Children in Need telethon (held once a year in November), and Comic Relief's Red Nose Day (held every two years in March). Some companies hold their own "fun days" to raise money for particular causes, as described in this lesson. On such fun days, employees are given licence to behave in a more relaxed way and to do silly things, such as the fundraising activities shown in the Picture Quiz on Page 2. Some employees don't want to get involved, perhaps because they object to this kind of institutionalised "fun" – being told by their bosses *when* they can have a good time. Or maybe because they prefer to keep their work life and social life separate. It may be that they don't want their colleagues or superiors (who may not be their friends) to see them in a more informal mood – or even in non-work clothes. In the

Pictures

Extensions: SS describe the pictures and how they are related to the lesson. SS look for other relevant pictures on the internet.

1 Dialogue – Parts 1-3

SS should be encouraged to work in pairs and practise their pronunciation by reading each dialogue out loud. It would be better to work through the lesson in sequence, rather than reading the dialogues together. There may be some unfamiliar vocabulary and expressions, including examples of colloquial speech, e.g. "I reckon…", "Are you gonna…?" and "party pooper" in Dialogue 1. SS could use their dictionaries or the teacher could pre-teach such vocabulary. SS could look online for further audible examples of sarcasm, e.g. in films, TV shows, as well as in everyday life, then play them back to the rest of the class. SS could have their own sarcastic conversations with each other – if they are not doing so already!

Extensions: See Talk a Lot Elementary Handbook for more ideas and guidance on developing dialogues and role plays. One tip is to add more detail to the scene. SS could invent more information about each character, e.g. what is the relationship between Keisha and Jack? We know they work in HR, but what are their roles? What did they have for breakfast this morning? Even trivial details can make the characters come alive, for example, perhaps Jack woke up late and didn't have time for breakfast, which put him in a bad mood. SS work together to add layers of detail which make the role plays much richer. SS could imagine what happened before Dialogue 1 and after Dialogue 3 – did they go out for a drink? – as well as what happens in between the dialogues. Of course, there are no right or wrong answers here: the idea is for SS to use their imaginations and to create something that can be assessed by the teacher in terms of spoken English, pronunciation, use of English, vocabulary, and so on.

2 Discussion Words & Pronunciation Focus

a) Stressed syllables are shown in blue type.
b) The suffixes are underlined:

Manage<u>ment</u>, Hum<u>an</u> Re<u>sour</u>ces (HR), Finance, Le<u>gal</u>, Sales, Mar<u>ket</u>ing, Pro<u>duc</u>tion, Distri<u>bu</u>tion, Infor<u>ma</u>tion Tech<u>nol</u>ogy (IT), Research and Develop<u>ment</u> (R&D), Custom<u>er</u> Ser<u>vice</u>, Mainte<u>nance</u>.

Extensions: Use the Discussion Word Questions from Talk a Lot Elementary Books 1-3 or Talk a Lot Intermediate Book 1, or use the Big Word Game or Talk a Lot Bingo from Talk a Lot Elementary Handbook. There is also related practice on the topic of suffixes in the Handbook. You could ask SS to think of more examples of departments in a company, or research different companies online and find out what departments they have – and what they do. SS could think about which departments are necessary in different-sized companies, e.g. small, medium, large, and multinational. SS could discuss working for a company department, if they have this kind of experience.

3 Information Exchange

Here is the completed grid, including answers to the Listening task (Exercise 7):

Department	1 Main Responsibilities	2 Funds Raised (8am - 1pm)	3 Funds Raised (1 - 4pm)	4 Funds Raised (Dept. Total)
Management	planning the way forward; troubleshooting	£467.13	£130.25	£597.38
Human Resources (HR)	finding new staff; caring for employees' needs; training	£228.10	£102.47	£330.57
Finance	payroll; doing the accounts	£104.35	£66.40	£170.75
Legal	dealing with legal issues; giving legal advice	£249.79	£156.79	£406.58
Sales	selling the products	£580.23	£246.18	£826.41
Marketing	making sure customers know about the products	£779.12	£482.97	**£1,262.09**
Production	manufacturing the products	£668.43	£422.44	£1,090.87
Distribution	getting the products in front of customers	£454.56	£234.68	£689.24
Information Technology (IT)	providing and maintaining computer equipment and software	£547.90	£108.61	£656.51
Research and Development (R&D)	coming up with new products	£487.19	£216.88	£704.07
Customer Service	ensuring the customer is happy and will order again	£640.53	£240.02	£880.55
Maintenance	taking care of equipment, property, and vehicles	£833.86	£427.90	£1,261.76
			Total Raised:	**£8,876.78**

a) The Maintenance Department has raised the most before lunch. Reasons will vary, for example, perhaps it is a big department, or perhaps they did some daring stunts, or provided the most interesting fundraising activities.
b) Answers will vary.

Extensions: You could ask SS to think about the results of the morning's fundraising. Why did the Finance Department raise the least? Perhaps because there are usually fewer employees in this department than in other departments; or because they are used to encouraging people to be frugal with money, so the role of fundraising doesn't come naturally to them...? Why did the Marketing Department raise much more? Perhaps because there are more employees, or the employees in this department are more creative and gifted at persuading people to take action – and so on.

SS could do the activity again with a different partner, taking the other role, e.g. A if they were B, and vice versa. Or repeat the activity using different figures, e.g. higher or lower amounts raised, or different department names. Or you could encourage SS to write their own definitions of what the company departments do, before beginning the information exchange activity.

SS could focus on question forms and write down the questions they used to get the missing information, e.g. for completing column 1 SS need to ask: "What are the main responsibilities of the _____ Department?" or "What does the _____ Department do?" etc. To complete column 2, SS need to ask: "How much did the _____ Department raise between 8am and 1pm?" or "...in the morning?" or something similar. You could encourage SS to think of some comparative/superlative questions and answers too, e.g.

"The _____ Department raised more than the _____ Department, but the _____ Department raised the most."

or, if the SS enjoy maths problems: "The _____ Department raised £_____ more/less than the _____ Department, etc.

Picture Quiz – Fundraising Activities

1. d)   2. a)   3. c)   4. b)

Extensions: SS research online and find out about each kind of activity – adding more that they know of. They could watch videos and swap accounts of their own fundraising initiatives. SS might be so inspired by this lesson that they decide to organise their own Fun Day in aid of a good cause – and actually take part in some of the activities discussed!

5 Non-Literal English – Oxymorons

The eight other oxymorons are below. Each phrase is a contradiction in terms, because the first word disagrees with the second word. While the phrases don't make sense literally, they work as idioms because each has a fixed meaning.

Dialogue 1:

Oxymoron:	Literal Meaning:	Where's the Contradiction?
It's a definite maybe	I'll think about it; I might come; it's a possibility	if something is definite, then there is no doubt about it – there is no maybe!

Dialogue 2:

Oxymoron:	Literal Meaning:	Where's the Contradiction?
it's the same difference to me	it doesn't matter to me either way; I'm not bothered; I don't mind	the same and difference are two opposite concepts
it's an open secret	it's officially a secret, but everybody knows about it	if something is open then by definition it cannot be secret
a bit of a minor disaster	a failure; a problem; something that didn't work out	something minor is fairly small, while a disaster is a very big problem
completely destroyed	ruined; totally destroyed	something complete is whole, while something destroyed is broken apart

Dialogue 3:

Oxymoron:	Literal Meaning:	Where's the Contradiction?
a social outcast	a person that other people don't want to know	social means "with others" while an outcast doesn't spend time with other people
an eloquent silence	when I don't speak it indicates more than if I replied	when somebody is eloquent they speak very well, while there is silence when nobody speaks
almost always	usually; most of the time; nine times out of ten	almost indicates a non-definite time period, while always indicates a definite time period

Extensions: SS could use each oxymoron in a new sentence, or make up a new dialogue that includes many or all of them. Or look for more oxymorons and think about how to apply them in an everyday conversation. SS might even have fun making up their own oxymorons, taking two opposite concepts and putting them together in a phrase. (For more examples of oxymorons, please see the worksheet "100 Great English Oxymorons" on page 5 of this pack.)

6 Listening – Track 1.3a

You can download the recordings for the lesson here:

Track 1.3a (full audio): https://purlandtraining.com/tali2-track1.3a.mp3
Track 1.3b (voice only – without sound effects): https://purlandtraining.com/tali2-track1.3b.mp3

See completed grid (above) for all the amounts raised.

a) The Marketing Department has raised the most funds for charity.
b) The company has raised £8,876.78 in total.

Extensions: SS read the transcript and study the new vocabulary and expressions – which could be tested in the next lesson. SS could write and read out their own final speech giving the same results as in the audio, or the teacher could read out the address, but change the amounts raised – to provide further practice of listening for numbers. Or SS write and read out an address given by Bernard Good at *lunchtime*, which announces the morning fundraising results and encourages the employees to raise even more money. Or SS could imagine Jack and Keisha's sarcastic commentary as they listen to Bernard Good's address – the teacher plays the audio file, while SS improvise their comments over the top.

The aim of any Talk a Lot course is for students to practise and improve their speaking, listening, and pronunciation skills. Along the way the student will learn plenty of new vocabulary – including non-literal English expressions, such as idioms, phrasal verbs, and slang – and also practise reading, writing, and grammar skills, e.g. verb forms, word order, parts of a sentence, and so on.

This two-page spread provides an organised sequence of learning activities for students at intermediate level (CEF B2). We believe that there is easily enough material here for a 90-minute lesson. Of course, how long the material lasts will depend on a variety of factors, such as the level of your students, and how familiar they are with Talk a Lot techniques. If you used any or all of the extension activities, you could make the material last much longer.

Although many of the activities in this book can be used without having previously studied with Talk a Lot material, e.g. the reading comprehension tests, this is the second Talk a Lot Intermediate course book and the author has assumed that students will have some prior knowledge of Talk a Lot methodology, e.g. knowing how to make sentence blocks, and how to find the stressed syllables and sounds in a word or phrase; or how to read the New English Alphabet.

Time Travelling

1 Listening – Find 20 Differences

Work in groups of 4. Students C & D follow the text (introduction and first column) as A & B read the alternative text (see Notes). Students C & D listen and mark 10 differences between the texts. Then swap over – A & B follow the rest of the text and mark 10 more differences, as C & D read. Check any new vocabulary in your dictionaries.

Welcome to Time Travelling Job Swap – the reality show that lets YOU change jobs with an employee from the past! This week, Cro-Magnon hunter-gatherer Borag travels forward 15,000 years to become a supermarket checkout operator for a week.

We grabbed an exclusive interview with Borag, ahead of this week's episode. He spoke via a special time travel interpreter:

Why do you work?
I work to get food for my clan. If I didn't go out hunting, we wouldn't eat, so it's absolutely vital!

Why did you choose your present career path?
My father was a hunter-gatherer and he showed me the ropes: how to trap a bear in a cave; how to skin a reindeer; how to fish. Pretty much all the men in my clan go out hunting. If you're young, fit, and strong, you have to bring back food for the group.

Tell me about your role in the company. Does it offer you status, job security, job satisfaction, and promotion opportunities?
My specific role is to cut up the animals after they've been killed. I'm quite a valued member of the hunting team. My job is safe because I'm pretty handy with a knife! I get a lot of pleasure from my work – particularly when I'm eating the delicious results! I'd like to work my way up from apprentice to assistant butcher, but I'm happy for now.

What do you value in your job? What do you dislike?
I love being out in the open air – running; chasing wild beasts. I love the feeling of the rain on my back and the wind in my hair; the excitement of discovering a herd of bison or perhaps a baby woolly mammoth that's been separated from its mother. I hate it when we can't find anything to eat and we have to return to our clan and face them with empty hands.

Tell me about your colleagues.
We're a mixed group in terms of age and experience, but all are strong and dedicated to the job in hand. Whether we're harpooning fish or capturing wild horses, it's a team effort. You know that you're working together for the good of the whole clan. It's a great feeling!

Name: Borag the Brave
Age: 22
From: Southern France
Time: 13,120 BC
Job: Hunter-Gatherer

If you could change one thing about your job, what would it be?
Nothing really – I love my job. Although, we don't have weekends or holidays, as such, so I would love to have a bit more free time to spend with my wife and my three children. I'm away from home a lot – travelling for long periods at a time.

What are the working conditions like? (hours, salary, leave, perks, etc.)
We work when we have to – often from early morning till late at night. If we've had a really big kill, we might not have to work for a few days. If that happens we can rest, and we might pass the time making jewellery or painting pictures on the walls of our caves. We get paid in meat, so if we don't work we will go to sleep hungry for sure.

What is your ambition? Where would you like to be in five years' time?
Like I said before, I'm hoping to become an assistant butcher, but five years is too far ahead for me to think, really. The most important goal is to stay alive – and that means dodging wild animals, avoiding hypothermia and infections – and most importantly bringing back food for my clan.

If you could do any job in the world, what would it be?
I would say to be chief hunter in our clan! What an honour! Because they get to wrestle with wolves and bears – and everybody respects them.

If you could take on any job from history, what would it be?
Well, I'm swapping places this week with Lee, a young guy from Finchley. He works as a cashier in a supermarket, so I'm looking forward to my first shift tomorrow. Bring it on!

2 Discussion Questions

Work in pairs. Use the questions above to ask and answer questions about **your** *work.*

3 Discussion Words – Work

a) Find the following words and phrases in the text and circle them
b) Find the stressed syllable in each, and write the strong vowel sound:

ambition	status	working conditions
hours	perks	job security
job satisfaction	pleasure	role
career path	leave	promotion
salary	goal	colleagues

Borag is more used to fighting off starving wolves than scanning cereal packets and soup. How do you think he will get on?

JOB SWAP

4 Pronunciation

a) Look at the sentences from the text below. Mark the strong stresses.

1. it was nice to meet his friends there

2. Lee lives in a warm, dry flat

3. It's really made me think about why we work.

4. I had to wear this horrible uniform all day

b) Look at the unstressed syllables. How many Schwa sounds are there? How many short i sounds are there?

5 Sentence Blocks

Which wh- question words can be used with each sentence above? Practise making sentence blocks with your partner. Check the stress!

7 Reading

It's the end of the week on the checkout, and we've managed to catch five minutes with Borag, who looks completely fed up:

How did you get on?
Oh, it was too boring! Lee showed me the ropes, and **it was nice to meet his friends there**, but the actual work itself was tedious. I felt like a robot having to scan every product – and the queue of people seemed endless!

What were the main differences compared with your current job?
I found it really hard to sit still for such long periods of time. Also the repetitive nature of the job was really getting to me by the end. I couldn't cope with the lack of physical exercise. I mean, human beings have got legs! We're meant to move. Humans are among the greatest runners on the planet. I found myself clock-watching all day, and dealing with idiotic comments from customers who seemed to look down on me. **I had to wear this horrible uniform all day** and my line manager told me I had to have a bath before going to work. Where I come from it doesn't matter how you're dressed or whether you smell nice. For some reason here it's a big deal!

What surprised you the most?
I didn't expect to have to deal with a female boss! In my clan the women have to raise the little ones and guard the camp. It was quite hard being told what to do by a woman. Also I was surprised at how… well, how overweight and unfit people from your time are! In my time we haven't got a chance to become fat. We're always on the move – and usually because we're pursuing our food!

What did you enjoy the most?
It was good to feel safe – without the threat of a violent death every minute of the day.

8 Role Plays

a) Work with a partner or group to make the following role plays. b) Use the questions above to do a final interview with each time traveller at the end of the role play.

 a) Imagine what happens next week when Lee travels back to Borag's time
 b) Imagine what would happen if YOU swapped jobs with either Borag or Lee
 c) Imagine swapping places with any employee from history, for example, an **Aztec warrior**, a **courtier** in the palace of The Sun King, or a **chimney sweep** from Victorian England…

6 Discussion & Function Words

Fill in the missing function words in the text and discuss the **reasons why we work** with your partner. Order them from 1-15, where 1 is the most important reason and 15 is the least. What are **YOUR** main reasons for working?

<u>Why Do We Work?</u>

* to buy luxury items, e.g. **1.** _____ expensive holiday
* to pay **2.** _____ our own living space
* to help other people
* to achieve a higher status **3.** _____ our friends
* to be able to afford non-essential items, e.g. a better car
* to get money to buy food **4.** _____ drink
* because money gives **5.** _____ control over our destinies
* to be able to pay our bills, e.g. light, heat, insurance, etc.
* to spend time **6.** _____ other people and not be alone
* to save so that we have money when **7.** _____ need it
* so that we **8.** _____ become bored
* so that we can purchase essential items, e.g. furniture
* to challenge ourselves
* money allows us to **9.** _____ more independent
* for pride – **10.** ____ feel fulfilled by doing something we are good at

Lee lives in a warm, dry flat and he told me there are no wild beasts roaming the streets of England any more – so that gave me confidence and peace of mind.

Would you like to swap jobs permanently?
No thanks! I miss my wide open spaces and fresh air. The rolling valleys, the hills, the mountains, the thrill of the chase as a dozen reindeer gallop off in terror… swap that for sitting on a till all day, in a supermarket for six days a week? No chance! I'll take my time over yours any day of the week!

What will you take away from this experience?
It's really made me think about why we work. I mean, in my time it's really simple: you have to work to put food on the table; but in your time you seem to have invented loads of different motivations for going to work. You want to have a career and job satisfaction. You want to get paid more and buy more things. You always need a bigger house, a better car, a more exotic holiday, nicer furniture… You need to challenge yourselves, get promoted, achieve a higher status… But really it's all about just getting enough for food for our bodies and making a safe place to live… isn't it?

Next week: discover what happens when Lee (below) swaps his scanner and "Here to Help" badge for a long-handled spear and a joint of barbecued reindeer!

Find out whether he eats or gets eaten in next week's exciting episode of Time Travelling Job Swap!

21

1 Listening – Find 20 Differences

Alternative Text – Part 1

--✂--

Students **A** & **B** read the first part of the text with 10 differences – shown in **bold type.** Students C & D should underline each word that has changed, and if possible write the new word:

A or **B:** Time Travelling Job Swap

Welcome to Time Travelling Job **Swat** [Swap] – the reality show that lets YOU change jobs with an employee from the past! This week, Cro-Magnon hunter-gatherer Borag travels forward 15,000 years to become a supermarket checkout operator for a week. We grabbed an exclusive interview with Borag, ahead of this week's episode. He spoke via a special **tile** [time] travel interpreter:

A Why do you work?

B I work to get food for my clan. If I didn't go out hunting, we wouldn't eat, so it's absolutely vital!

A Why did you choose your present career **park** [path]?

B My father was a hunter-gatherer and he showed me the ropes: how to trap a bear in a cave; how to skin a reindeer; how to **fit** [fish]. Pretty much all the men in my clan go out hunting. If you're young, fit, and strong, you have to bring back food for the group.

A Tell me about your role in the company. Does it offer you status, job security, **jog** [job] satisfaction, and promotion opportunities?

B My specific role is to cut up the animals after they've been **kilt** [killed]. I'm quite a valued member of the hunting team. My job is safe because I'm pretty handy with a **nice** [knife]! I get a lot of pleasure from my work – particularly when I'm eating the delicious results! I'd like to work my way up from apprentice to assistant butcher, but I'm happy for now.

A What do you value in your job? What do you dislike?

B I love being **owl** [out] in the open air – running; chasing wild beasts. I love the feeling of the rain on my back and the wind in my hair; the excitement of discovering a **hurl** [herd] of bison or perhaps a baby woolly mammoth that's been separated from its mother. I hate it when we can't find anything to **each** [eat] and we have to return to our clan and face them with empty hands.

--✂--

Alternative Text – Part 2

---

*Students **C** & **D** read the rest of the text with 10 more differences – shown in **bold type**. Students A & B should underline each word that has changed, and if possible write the new word:*

C Tell me about your colleagues.

D We're a mixed group in terms of **aid** [age] and experience, but all are strong and dedicated to the job in hand. Whether we're harpooning fish or capturing wild horses, it's a team effort. You know that you're working together for the good of the **home** [whole] clan. It's a **grape** [great] feeling!

C If you could change one thing about your job, what would it be?

D Nothing really – I love my job. Although, we don't have weekends or holidays, as such, so I would love to have a bit more free time to spend with my wife and my three children. I'm away from home a lot – travelling for long periods at a time.

C What are the working conditions **light** [like]? (hours, salary, leave, perks, etc.)

D We work when we have to – often from early morning till late at night. If we've had a really big kill, we might not have to work for a few days. If that happens we can rest, and we might **part** [pass] the time making jewellery or painting pictures on the walls of our caves. We get paid in meat, so if we don't work we will go to sleep hungry for sure.

C What is your ambition? Where **wool** [would] you like to be in five years' time?

D Like I said before, I'm hoping to become an assistant butcher, but five years is too far ahead for me to **thing** [think], really. The most important goal is to stay alive – and that means dodging wild animals, avoiding hypothermia and infections – and most importantly bringing back food for my **clam** [clan].

C If you could do any job in the world, what would it be?

D I would say to be chief hunter in our clan! What an honour! Because they get to wrestle with wolves and bears – and everybody respects **then** [them].

C If you could take on any job from history, what would it be?

D Well, I'm swapping places this **wheat** [week] with Lee, a young guy from Finchley. He works as a cashier in a supermarket, so I'm looking forward to my first shift tomorrow. Bring it on!

Title

"Time Travelling Job Swap". This lesson is about a fictional TV show where people from the present day are able to exchange jobs with an individual from the past for a week to find out what their job was like. You could start by asking SS some warm-up questions, e.g. "What is your favourite period in history? Why?", "What jobs did they do in the past that we don't do today?", and "If you could travel back in time and try any job for one week, where would you go and what would you do? Why?" etc.

Pictures

Extensions: SS describe the pictures and how they are related to the lesson. SS look for other relevant pictures on the internet.

1 Listening – Find 20 Differences

See Alternative Text on P.3 for instructions. SS should check any new words and expressions in their dictionaries, or you could pre-teach any vocabulary that you think may be new before starting the activity. When SS have finished the activity and checked their answers, ask them what they notice about the words that were exchanged. They should notice that in each case the **final consonant sound** of each word has been changed to make a different word.

Extensions: a) SS could practise their speaking and listening skills by reading the interview in pairs, then changing roles and reading it again. b) They could repeat the listening activity but with different words changed, e.g. instead of final consonant sounds they could change the vowel sound in one-syllable words to make a different word, e.g. "get" changes to "got", "eat" to "ate", and so on.

2 Discussion Questions

SS should work in pairs and ask each other the ten questions from the text. SS should give answers about themselves. Here is the complete list:

1. Why do you work?
2. Why did you choose your present career path?
3. Tell me about your role in the company. Does it offer you status, job security, job satisfaction, and promotion opportunities?
4. What do you value in your job? What do you dislike?
5. Tell me about your colleagues.
6. If you could change one thing about your job, what would it be?
7. What are the working conditions like? (hours, salary, leave, perks, etc.)
8. What is your ambition? Where would you like to be in five years' time?
9. If you could do any job in the world, what would it be?
10. If you could take on [try; do; have a go at] any job from history, what would it be?

Extensions: SS could think of more questions on the topic of work. They could ask and answer the new questions either as themselves or as Borag. Or SS could conduct a survey by asking a variety of students from the class, and then compile their results into a short report which they then present to the class. To consolidate this, they could write out the report for homework.

3 Discussion Words – Work

SS should check any new words or phrases in their dictionaries. Here are the discussion words with stressed syllables underlined and strong vowel sounds indicated. The teaching point is that these strong vowel sounds are the most important sounds in each word or phrase, and therefore should be heard clearly.

i	ei	er
amb<u>i</u>tion	<u>sta</u>tus	w<u>or</u>king conditions

auw	er	uuw
<u>hours</u>	<u>perks</u>	job sec<u>u</u>rity

a	e	eu
job satis**fac**tion	**plea**sure	**role**
iy	ee	eu
ca**reer** path	**leave**	pro**mo**tion
a	eu	o
salary	**goal**	**col**leagues

Extensions: a) SS could match words and phrases that have the same strong-stressed vowel sound, i.e.

w<u>o</u>rking conditions *and* p<u>e</u>rks; r<u>o</u>le, pr<u>o</u>motion, *and* g<u>o</u>al; job satisf<u>a</u>ction *and* s<u>a</u>lary

b) SS could think of more discussion words on the topic of work and repeat the activity above; then use the words and phrases from the activity or the ones they have found (or both) to practise with any Discussion Words practice activities, i.e. from Talk a Lot Elementary Books 1-3 or Talk a Lot Intermediate Book 1. Or SS could use the Big Word Game or Talk a Lot Bingo from Talk a Lot Elementary Handbook. You could also get SS to put each word or phrase into a sentence, using a verb form of their (or your) choice, or to practise making collocations, e.g. verb and noun (<u>apply for</u> a promotion), or adjective and noun (a <u>high</u> salary), etc.

4 Pronunciation

a) The strong stresses are marked: O
b) Schwa sounds are marked: • ; short i sounds are marked: • ; other unstressed syllables are marked: o

NEA Phonetic Translation:

1. it was nice to meet his friends there   i_ w Znai st Mee ti Zfren Ztheir

2. Lee lives in a warm, dry flat   Lee Li vzi n Worm, Drai Flat

3. It's really made me think about why we work.   i_ Sriy lii Mei mi Tting k bau_ Wai wi Work.

4. I had to wear this horrible uniform all day   uh ha_ t Weir thi So r bl Yoo n for morl dei

SS should notice that the vowel sounds in the unstressed syllables in these sentences are mainly either Schwa sounds or short i sounds. This is true of unstressed syllables in an English sentence generally. Out of 22 unstressed sounds, there are **9 Schwa sounds**, **7 short i sounds**, and **6 other sounds**. Note: in sentence 1 the preposition "there", which is often an unstressed function word, is stressed because it occurs at the end of the sentence.

Extensions: SS examine other sentences from the text – or that they have made up on the same topic – to see how many Schwa sounds, short i sounds, and other sounds comprise the unstressed syllables.

5 Sentence Blocks

Note: parts of the text *in italics* will vary. SS should use their own ideas:

1. it was nice to meet his friends there (past simple)

Who was it nice to meet there? / His friends. / Was it nice to meet his friends there? / Yes, it was. / Was it nice to meet his *bank manager* there? / No, it wasn't. It wasn't nice to meet his *bank manager* there. / So…

What was it nice to do there? / To meet his friends. / Was it nice to meet his friends there? / Yes, it was. / Was it nice to *do your homework* there? / No, it wasn't. It wasn't nice to *do my homework* there. / So…

Where was it nice to meet his friends? / There. / Was it nice to meet his friends there? / Yes, it was. / Was it nice to meet his friends *in a crowded lift*? / No, it wasn't. It wasn't nice to meet his friends *in a crowded lift*. / So…

2. Lee lives in a warm, dry flat (present simple)

Who lives in a warm, dry flat? / Lee does. / Does Lee live in a warm, dry flat? / Yes, he does. / Does *a prisoner* live in a warm, dry flat? / No, they don't. *A prisoner* doesn't live in a warm, dry flat. / So…

Where does Lee live? / In a warm, dry flat. / Does Lee live in a warm, dry flat? / Yes, he does. / Does Lee live in a *cold, damp house*? / No, he doesn't. Lee doesn't live in a *cold, damp house*. / So…

What kind of flat does Lee live in? / A warm, dry one. / Does Lee live in a warm, dry flat? / Yes, he does. / Does Lee live in a *horrible* flat? / No, he doesn't. Lee doesn't live in a *horrible* flat. / So…

3. It's really made me think about why we work. (present perfect)

What has it really made you think about? / Why we work. / Has it really made you think about why we work? / Yes, it has. / Has it really made you think about *astrophysics*? / No, it hasn't. It hasn't really made me think about *astrophysics*. / So…

What has it really made you do? / Think about why we work. / Has it really made you think about why we work? / Yes, it has. / Has it really made you *feel annoyed*? / No, it hasn't. It hasn't really made me *feel annoyed*. / So…

4. I had to wear this horrible uniform all day (past modal form)

What did you have to wear all day? / This horrible uniform. / Did you have to wear that horrible uniform all day? / Yes, I did. / Did you have to wear *casual clothes* all day? / No, I didn't. I didn't have to wear *casual clothes* all day. / So…

What did you have to do all day? / Wear this horrible uniform. / Did you have to wear that horrible uniform all day? / Yes, I did. / Did you have to *stay in bed* all day? / No, I didn't. I didn't have to *stay in bed* all day. / So…

What kind of uniform did you have to wear all day? / This horrible uniform. / Did you have to wear that horrible uniform all day? / Yes, I did. / Did you have to wear *a nice* uniform all day? / No, I didn't. I didn't have to wear *a nice* uniform all day. / So…

Who had to wear that horrible uniform all day? / I did. / Did you have to wear that horrible uniform all day? / Yes, I did. / Did *your niece* have to wear that horrible uniform all day? / No, she didn't. *My niece* didn't have to wear this horrible uniform all day. / So…

How long did you have to wear that horrible uniform for? / All day. / Did you have to wear that horrible uniform all day? / Yes, I did. / Did you have to wear that horrible uniform *for only a few hours*? / No, I didn't. I didn't have to wear this horrible uniform *for only a few hours*. / So…

Extensions: Use other sentences from the text (or sentences written by SS on the same topic) and practise building sentence blocks using a variety of question words. SS can work individually, in pairs, in small groups, or as a whole class. See Talk a Lot Elementary Handbook for further ideas.

6 Discussion & Function Words

1. an
2. for
3. than
4. and
5. us
6. with
7. we
8. don't

9. be
10. to

SS should discuss the reasons and put them into order from 1 (most important) to 15 (least important). There are no right or wrong answers here. SS could present the results of their discussion to the whole class. Or SS could interview each other – even recording the interviews (audio or video), where possible. SS could work in small groups or pairs and leave the classroom to go and find a group of employees to interview on the topic of "Why Do We Work?" – e.g. at the school, or at a company, then come back and edit their interviews together, and show them to the whole group.

7 Reading

SS should read the interview out loud with a partner, then change roles and read it again. They should check any new words and expressions in their dictionaries, or you could pre-teach any vocabulary that you think might be new before starting the activity. The reading may lead into a discussion about Borag's attitudes towards work and the present day, and how they contrast with our modern attitudes – or it may lead directly into the role play activity.

8 Role Plays

Extensions: See Talk a Lot Elementary Handbook for more ideas and guidance on developing role plays. One tip is to start to add more detail to the scene. SS could invent more information about each character, e.g. we don't know much about the character of Lee from the text, so students could flesh it out a bit. As SS work together to add layers of detail the role play will become much richer. Of course, there are no right or wrong answers here: the idea is for SS to use their imaginations and to create something that can be assessed by the teacher in terms of spoken English, pronunciation, use of English, vocabulary, and so on. If your SS are competitive, there could be a challenge between groups to see which produces the most professional role play. SS could record their performances on video, and since the lesson is based on a fictional TV show, it could be a good chance for SS to learn how to create and edit a short video in the style of a reality show (e.g. *Undercover Boss*). If the performances are particularly good, you could invite people from within your school (e.g. other classes or staff) and even people from outside the school (parents, friends, etc.) to watch the resulting work, as a form of promotion for your school.

*English is a rich language, which means there is often more than one way to say exactly the same thing. Native speakers often enjoy using idioms, phrasal verbs, and slang – a kind of **picture language** – rather than literal dictionary words, because it feels more natural to them. When speech includes a lot of this kind of non-literal English, as in the dialogues below, it can be really confusing for the English student, who might feel as if they're not listening to English at all, but…*

A DIFFERENT LANGUAGE

1 Dialogue 1 – Quiz

a) Read the dialogue with your partner quickly to get the gist. Student A is **Leanna** and Student B is **Billie**.
Note that the dialogues in this lesson are not exaggerated – native speakers (especially young people) really do speak like this!
b) Read it together more slowly. Each student reads their lines and tells or guesses the **literal translation** of each idiomatic phrase in red type. The other student checks the meaning on their handout (see PP.3-4) and gives 10 points for each correct answer. The student with the most points is the winner!

Two teenage girls are chatting on the bus…

L: ¹Why the long face? ² What's up?
B: Brandon's ³ chucked me.
L: What?
B: Yeah. We had ⁴ a bust-up last night – at Kim's party – and he's been ⁵ giving me the cold shoulder ever since.
L: Ah! You must be ⁶ gutted.
B: I'll ⁷ get over it, I suppose.
L: What was it about?
B: Well, you know, at first I thought he was ⁸ playing hard to get. Then when we started ⁹ going out he was still ¹⁰ putting it about with some girl from the school play, which was really ¹¹ winding me up.
L: Yeah. I remember.
B: So, yesterday afternoon I was shopping in town when I saw Brandon walking hand in hand with ¹² a right minger who works in the fish and chip shop – who's actually ¹³ got a bun in the oven anyway by *another* ¹⁴ complete lowlife!
L: Ah, babe. ¹⁵ I'm lost for words. Well, ¹⁶ it's not the end of the world, is it? ¹⁷ Plenty more fish in the sea, and all that. I reckon you're better off ¹⁸ well rid.
B: I'd love to ¹⁹ teach him a lesson though.
L: ²⁰ Don't stoop to his level. You know – just ²¹ pick up the pieces and ²² move on with your life. ²³ Be the better person.
B: D'you ever get the feeling that ²⁴ life sucks? I really trusted him, you know. How could he just ²⁵ stab me in the back like that? And he's so ²⁶ two-faced! I thought we were ²⁷ soul mates – together forever! I know I ²⁸ took him for granted sometimes, but…
L: I guess you just ²⁹ don't know what you've got till it's gone.

"She's got a bun in the oven" –
not connected with buns… or ovens

c) Read the dialogue again, but this time replace the idiomatic phrases with the literal ones. Do you notice any difference? Which way is easier to understand? Which way is more interesting?

2 True, False, or Unknown?

Work in pairs and mark each statement T, F, or U:

1. Billie has split up with her boyfriend.
2. Leanna encourages Billie to get back with Brandon.
3. Leanna went to Kim's party last night.
4. Billie's not bothered about the break-up.
5. Brandon was unfaithful to Billie with a girl who works in a fast food place.
6. Billie is not bitter about what's happened.
7. Billie and Leanna are best friends.
8. Billie thought that the relationship had a future.

3 Non-Literal English – Clichés

A cliché is a standard phrase (often an idiom) that we use to express a feeling when we can't think of the words on our own – or when we are too lazy to think of our own phrase.

Clichés are, by definition, unoriginal and over-used. We often reach for a cliché when we need to react to some important news, e.g. a life-changing event or decision. For example, in Dialogue 1, above, the following phrases are clichés:

"just pick up the pieces and move on with your life"
"I guess you just don't know what you've got till it's gone"

Leanna uses clichés to give advice; perhaps because she has heard them before (e.g. on a TV talk show or soap opera) and believes that they sound like the right thing to say.

a) Find two more clichéd phrases in Dialogue 1 and two more in Dialogue 2 on the opposite page
b) Can you think of any more clichés that the girls could use in this situation?

4 Pronunciation – Final t Sound (Tracks 2.1a & 2.1b)

1. not nice
2. what was
3. can't believe
4. get the
5. don't know
6. got with
7. that life
8. what they

a) Find the phrases above in the dialogues and circle them
b) Repeat the phrases a few times with your partner
c) Listen to Track 2.1a, then Track 2.1b. The phrases are said in two different ways. What is the difference? Which way sounds more like natural English? Which way would you normally say them?
d) Listen again to the second way (Track 2.1.b) and repeat the phrases
e) Find more examples in the dialogue of similar phrases, where a t sound at the end of a syllable meets a consonant sound at the beginning of the next, and practise saying them in the manner that you heard in Track 2.1b

"He was playing the field" – not discussing an actual field

Some frustrated students speak out:

"It sounds like they're discussing relationship problems, so why do I hear nouns like bell, fish, trousers, oven, and so on? Why can't they say what they mean?"

[Answer: because English is not a direct language!"]

"When I hear the word fish I picture it and imagine it with its literal meaning; I get confused because I haven't yet learned that 'plenty more fish in the sea' is an idiom – a phrase with a fixed meaning. I need to learn more idioms!"

5 Dialogue 2 – Quiz

Follow the same instructions as for Dialogue 1. Student A is **Leanna** and Student B is **Terri**. Next, work together to create a short dialogue using 10 of the new idiomatic phrases from this lesson, and perform it to the rest of the class.

L: Have you heard ¹the latest about Billie?
T: What?
L: She's had a massive ²argy-bargy with Brandon! He's ³gone off with ⁴some scrubber from the ⁵chippie.
T: ⁶You're joking! Well, he's ⁷led her a merry dance, hasn't he? The ⁸low-down, rotten scum. Talk about being ⁹done over! She was ¹⁰so totally into him, wasn't she?
L: I know, but anyway – ¹¹I reckon she was punching above her weight a bit, don't you think? And anyway, Brandon was ¹²playing the field with a bunch of ¹³old flames, the whole time he and Billie were ¹⁴an item. His mates were ¹⁵blabbing their mouths off that he was having ¹⁶a bit on the side when he first ¹⁷got with Billie.
T: Oh, you can't believe a word of what *they* say. I'd ¹⁸take it with a pinch of salt, if I were you. They're ¹⁹all mouth and trousers. How's Billie? ²⁰Keeping her chin up?
L: Pretty ²¹down in the dumps, really. I think she's just ²²sick and tired of ²³hooking up with ²⁴jerks. It's not nice being ²⁵cheated on, is it? I mean – her previous ²⁶bf was ²⁷a total loser too, wasn't he?
T: I know, but anyway… Ah, ²⁸bless her. You know, we need to get her ²⁹all dolled up. Tell her to ³⁰get her glad rags on and ³¹her dancing shoes as well, and we'll take her out for ³²a night on the town. She can ³³paint the town red and just ³⁴let her hair down. Some ³⁵sick music'll be ³⁶just the trick to ³⁷mend her broken heart.
L: Yeah. Great idea! Let's ³⁸give her a bell and ³⁹see how she's fixed for tonight.

Discuss with your partner and then with the whole class: how can we learn MORE non-literal English?

"There's plenty more fish in the sea" – not about counting marine life

6 Discussion Words – NEA Translation

a) Say the words from Dialogue 2 (below) out loud. Where is the strong stress? What is the strong vowel sound? Are there any Schwa sounds or short i sounds? Are there any silent letters?

massive   dance   mates   mouths

give   fixed   trousers   tonight

b) Match them with their NEA translations:

t Nait   Mauthz   Fikst   Giv   Trau zz   Meits   Ma siv   Darns

c) Translate 10 more **content words** from the dialogues into the NEA and then repeat exercise a) above

7 Sentence Blocks

Work in pairs. Make the six sentence blocks:

BRANDON WAS PLAYING THE FIELD WITH A BUNCH OF OLD FLAMES, THE WHOLE TIME HE AND BILLIE WERE AN ITEM.

when, who (x2), what (x2), how long

29

1 Dialogue 1 – Quiz

--✂---

Student A checks as **Student B** tells or guesses Billie's literal translations:

[3] ended our relationship
[4] an argument
[5] ignoring me
[7] recover
[8] deliberately making it hard for me to get close to him
[9] having a romantic relationship
[10] in a close relationship
[11] annoying me
[12] a really ugly girl
[13] pregnant
[14] horrible guy
[19] do something nasty to him so that he regrets hurting me
[24] life is horrible
[25] betray me
[26] deceitful
[27] two people who matched perfectly
[28] didn't appreciate him fully

--✂---

Student B checks as **Student A** tells or guesses Leanna's literal translations:

[1] Why do you look so sad?
[2] What's wrong?
[6] really upset.
[15] I don't know what to say
[16] it's not that serious
[17] There are lots of other potential partners around
[18] without him
[20] Don't behave as badly as he has
[21] recover gradually
[22] forget the past and focus on a more positive future
[23] Act like a more morally superior person than him
[29] don't value what you have until you have lost it

--✂---

5 Dialogue 2 – Quiz

------------------------------✂------------------------------

Student A checks as **Student B** tells or guesses Terri's literal translations:

[6] Is that really true?
[7] treated her very badly
[8] very bad person
[9] betrayed
[10] very keen on him
[18] treat it as if it were not true
[19] always boasting about relationships
[20] staying positive
[28] I wish her well
[29] dressed up smartly
[30] put on her best party clothes
[31] shoes which are suitable for dancing
[32] a night at some pubs and clubs in town
[33] have a good time with friends, visiting pubs and nightclubs
[34] relax
[35] very good
[36] the best way
[37] help her to recover after being hurt emotionally

------------------------------✂------------------------------

Student B checks as **Student A** tells or guesses Leanna's literal translations:

[1] the latest news
[2] fight
[3] started to date
[4] an unpleasant woman
[5] fish and chip shop
[11] I think that she had a lower social status than him
[12] having romantic relationships
[13] former partners
[14] together in an exclusive relationship
[15] boasting
[16] a secret relationship
[17] started to date
[21] unhappy
[22] very tired of
[23] starting relationships
[24] idiots
[25] deceived by your partner, who is having a relationship with somebody else at the same time as you
[26] boyfriend
[27] an unpleasant person
[38] call her
[39] see whether she's available

------------------------------✂------------------------------

Foundation Course

Lesson 2 – 200 One-Syllable Words that End with "t"

Practise making **glottal stops** *with this handy list of one-syllable words that end with t :*

ant	dote	mart	sat	wrote
art	fat	mat	seat	wrought
at	fate	mate	set	yacht
bait	feat	Matt	short	yet
Bart	feet	meat	shot	zit
bat	fight	meet	sight	
beat	fit	met	sit	
beet	fleet	might	skate	*My words:*
belt	float	mitt	soot	
bet	foot	moat	sot	_____
bit	fought	mutt	sought	
bite	gate	Nate	splat	_____
bleat	get	neat	spout	
blot	git	net	sprout	_____
boat	gnat	newt	start	
bolt	goat	night	stat	_____
boot	got	nit	state	
bought	greet	not	stoat	_____
brat	grit	note	straight	
Brit	grot	nought	tart	_____
brought	gut	nut	tat	
built	hart	oat	Tate	_____
but	hat	ought	taught	
butt	hate	part	thought	_____
cart	heart	pat	throat	
cat	heat	peat	tight	_____
caught	height	pert	tit	
cert	hit	pet	toot	_____
chart	hot	Pete	tot	
chat	hurt	pit	tote	_____
cheat	hut	plate	treat	
chute	it	pleat	tut	_____
clot	jet	port	vat	
coat	jot	pot	vet	_____
coot	jut	put	vote	
cot	jute	quit	wait	_____
crate	Kate	quite	wart	
curt	kit	quote	weight	_____
cut	kite	rat	wet	
cute	late	rate	what	_____
dart	let	rent	wheat	
date	light	right	white	_____
debt	lit	root	wilt	
dirt	loot	rot	wit	_____
dot	lot	rut	writ	

Practise glottal stops by repeating these four fun phrases – then make up some of your own!

- Kate wrote a short note.
- Bart bought some light wheat.
- The goat with the neat coat met a stoat whose feet got hot a lot.
- Pete's pet cat knew a neat newt.

Title

"A Different Language". The aim of this lesson is to explore how English can sound like a different language when native speakers use a lot of non-literal expressions. In the dialogues from this lesson, SS can learn (or revise) **68 different idiomatic expressions** on the topic of relationships. SS should focus on the idiomatic language in the dialogues, and how idioms include words which have no connection with their normal literal meaning, for example, in the idiom "he's been giving me the cold shoulder", the meaning ("he's been ignoring me") is unconnected with the words "cold" and "shoulder". But if SS don't know the idiom, the use of these unrelated words can make them picture only the literal meaning of each word. Of course, the answer is for SS to first of all be aware that we use idioms and non-literal language in English, and secondly to learn idioms in a regular, systematic way, like they would learn any vocabulary. On page 2 of the lesson there are some "student complaints": "…so why do I hear nouns like bell, fish, trousers, oven, and so on?" Here is a full list of nouns (in order) which are used in a non-literal way in the dialogues:

Dialogue 1: shoulder, bun, oven, world, fish, sea, lesson, level, pieces, back, soul, mates

Dialogue 2: scrubber, dance, scum, weight, flames, item, mouths, bit, side, pinch, salt, mouth, trousers, chin, dumps, jerks, rags, dancing, shoes, hair, trick, heart, bell

Pictures

Extensions: SS describe the pictures and how they are related to the lesson. SS look for other relevant pictures on the internet.

1 Dialogue 1 – Quiz

c) SS' answers will vary and a short class discussion could develop. Hopefully SS will realise that there is a big difference when we use idiomatic phrases instead of literal ones. While using literal phrases may be easier for SS to understand – because they have already learned them in class – using idiomatic phrases makes the dialogue more interesting – and also closer to how an actual conversation between two native speakers would be.

Extensions: a) You could make this exercise more difficult by not giving the SS the handouts with the answers on. Instead they have to use dictionaries (e.g. a dictionary of idioms) or the internet to find the literal meanings, and then write their own literal version of the dialogue. b) After completing the exercise, SS could work in pairs or small groups and develop a short role play based on what they imagine was happening before the dialogue began, or what happened afterwards, or spend time looking for more idioms and slang expressions on the topic of love and relationships.

2 True, False, or Unknown?

Where possible, encourage SS to tell you a sentence from the dialogue to back up their answer, rather than giving just a letter:

    1. T   "Brandon's chucked me."
    2. F   "…it's not the end of the world, is it?"
    3. U   We don't know because this information is not given in the dialogue.
    4. F   "Why the long face? What's up?"
    5. T   "…I saw Brandon walking hand in hand with a right minger who works in the fish and chip shop."
    6. F   "I'd love to teach him a lesson though."
    7. U   We don't know because this information is not given in the dialogue. Perhaps not, considering how Leanna speaks to Terri about Billie in Dialogue 2.
    8. T   "I thought we were soul mates – together forever!"

Extensions: SS could make up further statements where the answer is true, false, or unknown, and test their partners. SS could use some of the sentences (not the negative ones) as starting sentences for building sentence blocks, e.g. "Billie has split up with her boyfriend. / WHO has split up…" etc.

3 Non-Literal English – Clichés

a) Since Leanna and Billie include a lot of well-known standard phrases (idioms) in their dialogues, it is fair to say that much of their speech is clichéd. However, the following phrases stand out as being particularly clichéd:

Dialogue 1:

"I'm lost for words."
"It's not the end of the world, is it?"
"Plenty more fish in the sea, and all that."
"Don't stoop to his level."

Dialogue 2:

"He's led her a merry dance, hasn't he?"
"I'd take it with a pinch of salt, if I were you."
"Tell her to get her glad rags on and her dancing shoes as well…"
"She can paint the town red and just let her hair down."

b) SS' answers will vary. For example, other clichés (idioms that apply very generally to a situation) that could be used include:

Billie says:

"I need time *to get over him*…" (to recover from being hurt)
"I felt we were *made for each other*…" (a perfect couple)
"*It's hit me like a ton of bricks*…" (it has been a big shock)
"It's completely *out of the blue*…" (unexpected)

Leanna says:

"*You're better off without him*…" (your life will be better without him)
"*Just put it down to experience*…" (see it as something that has given you more experience of life)
"Try to *put it behind you*…" (forget the past and focus on a more positive future)

Extensions: SS could look for more examples of clichéd language in online videos, e.g. on YouTube, or on DVDs, in songs, and so on. SS could then try to rewrite lines which contain clichés using their own original phrases instead.

4 Pronunciation – Final t Sound (Tracks 2.1a & 2.1b)

You can download the recordings for the lesson here:

Track 2.1a: https://purlandtraining.com/tali2-track2.1a.mp3
Track 2.1b: https://purlandtraining.com/tali2-track2.1b.mp3

c) SS should be able to hear that the phrases in the second recording (Track 2.1b) sound more natural than those in the first (Track 2.1a). The reason for this is that in Track 2.1b the speaker uses elision to remove the t sound at the end of the first syllable, and adds a glottal stop before the next sound, whereas in Track 2.1a the speaker pronounces the t sound. This sounds awkward next to the following consonant sound, because it is a cc (consonant to consonant) sound connection, rather than the more usual and more natural-sounding vc (vowel to consonant) sound connection. You can see how the glottal stops (marked with _) have replaced the final t sound in the NEA phonetic spelling of the phrases below:

Normal Spelling: NEA Translation:

1. not nice   No_ Nais
2. what was   Wo_ wz
3. can't believe   Karn_ b Leev
4. get the   Ge_ th
5. don't know   Deun_ Neu
6. got with   Go_ with
7. that life   th_ Laif
8. what they   wo_ thei

This could be a good opportunity to revise (or study for the first time) how the glottal stop is used in English. You can find more information on this topic in *Talk a Lot Foundation Course*, which is a free download from purlandtraining.com. Read *Lesson 2 – Spelling and Sounds* in particular, and allow SS time to practise forming the glottal stop. On page 19 of this lesson there is a list of 200 one-syllable words that end with a t sound, which can provide plenty of practice of making glottal stops. It is included in this pack on page 5. There are also plenty of videos online which demonstrate how to make the glottal stop. Note: syllable linking and connected speech in general is covered in detail in *Unit 4* of *Talk a Lot Foundation Course*. If SS ask why they have to study this, it could be worth pointing out to them that the final t sound – and consequently the elision and glottal stop combination – is very common in spoken English – **there are 65 final t sounds in these two short dialogues!** – so it is really important to study it if they want to achieve a more natural-sounding spoken English.

e) There are many more similar phrases in the dialogues, for example:

Normal Spelling:	NEA Translation:
wasn't she?	Wo zn_ shi?
don't you	Deun_ y
thought we	Ttor_ wi

SS should avoid phrases where the first syllable ends with a consonant cluster, rather than a single t sound. There are several phrases, for example, where the first syllable ends with st . If this happens, elision may or may not occur but a glottal stop is unnecessary. Instead, we use FCL (final consonant linking) and the consonant cluster st moves forward to the beginning of the next syllable, for example:

elision does not occur and there is no glottal stop:

| just don't | ju Steunt |
| just stab | ju Stab |

elision occurs, but there is no glottal stop:

just sick	ju Sik
just chill	ju Schil
just the	ju sth

There are also a few phrases where a final t sound meets another consonant sound and the t sound is kept, but the sound at the beginning of the next syllable disappears (using elision), for example:

| thought he | Ttor ti |
| hasn't he? | Ha zn_ tee? |

Extensions: a) SS could record themselves practising the phrases, or new phrases that they have found from the dialogues – or any examples of cc sound connections where a final t sound meets another consonant sound. SS listen back to each other's recordings and offer feedback. Of course, the teacher should also offer feedback to each student. If possible SS should record themselves saying the phrases **on video** so that they can watch how they physically make the sounds, e.g. what position the mouth and tongue are in. b) SS could extend the phrases into full sentences and practise saying them, paying particular attention to the cc sound connection, e.g. after practising "not nice, not nice," etc. SS should practise the phrase in its wider context: "It's not nice being cheated on." etc.

5 Dialogue 2 – Quiz

SS should follow the same instructions as for Dialogue 1. They can use some or all of the same extensions as well – or think up their own.

Discussion question: **"How can we learn MORE non-literal English?"**

SS should think of their own list of ways in which they can learn more non-literal English, but here are a few suggestions to get the discussion started:

In general, SS should try to immerse themselves in the English language as much as possible. The following tips will help them to learn more non-literal English in context:

- buy a dictionary of English idioms and resolve to learn 10 new idioms per week in a systematic way. Do the

- same for phrasal verbs, and even for slang too
- read English language websites, e.g. newspapers, gossip sites, information sites, etc.
- make friends with an English native speaker and chat on Skype or email each other
- watch English-language films with English subtitles on YouTube
- read the comments that people leave on YouTube, or similar sites, and look up any new idioms, phrasal verbs, and slang
- watch DVDs and films on TV with English subtitles
- exchange messages with English native speaker friends on Facebook
- attend free English lessons online at websites such as WizIQ.com
- pay for lessons with an English native speaker, e.g. on Skype, and focus on non-literal English
- use Twitter in English and read what people are tweeting on a particular topic
- spend time in the UK – either for a short holiday or for a longer stay
- learn English or work in the UK or an English-speaking country

6 Discussion Words – NEA (New English Alphabet) Translation

a) SS should check any new words or phrases in their dictionaries. Here are the discussion words with stressed syllables <u>underlined</u> and strong vowel sounds indicated.

a	ar	ei	au	i	i	au	ai
<u>ma</u>ssive	dance	mates	mouths	give	fixed	<u>trou</u>sers	to<u>night</u>

There are Schwa sounds in the following words: trous<u>e</u>rs, t<u>o</u>night

There are short i sounds in the following words: mass<u>i</u>ve, g<u>i</u>ve, f<u>i</u>xed

There are silent letters (letters which are not pronounced) in every word: mas<u>s</u>ive, danc<u>e</u>, mat<u>e</u>s, giv<u>e</u>, fix<u>e</u>d, trous<u>e</u>rs, toni<u>gh</u>t

b) Normal Spelling: NEA Translation:

   massive   Ma siv
   dance   Darns
   mates   Meits
   mouths   Mauthz
   give   Giv
   fixed   Fikst
   trousers   Trau zz
   tonight   t Nait

c) Here are some more examples of content words (nouns, main verbs, adjectives, etc.) from the dialogues translated into the NEA:

   Normal Spelling: NEA Translation:

   face   Feis
   shopping   Sho ping
   pieces   Pee sz
   believe   b Leev
   broken   Breu kn

Extensions: a) SS could look at the NEA in more detail, if they are not already familiar with it (see *Talk a Lot Foundation Course Page 16* for the full chart and *Lesson 2 Page 6* for more information) and practise using it to write simple one- or two-syllable words, for example their first name or their friends' names. SS could discuss the differences between the NEA and other phonetic alphabets, and consider whether their dictionary has phonetic spellings of the words it contains and how this could help them to understand the differences between spelling and sounds in English. If SS are familiar with the NEA, you could have a team writing race activity, where two teams compete to see which can write a given word (e.g. a word from this lesson) on the board using the NEA. Or SS have to write a word on the board and their team has to shout out the normal English spelling, and so on. b) You could also use this activity as an opportunity to discuss the Schwa sound, or the short i sound (which is sometimes called "the second Schwa sound" because it is a very short sound which is consequently found in many unstressed syllables), or stress and strong vowel sounds, or silent letters – whichever of these topics your SS are currently least confident in. c) SS could think of more discussion words on the topic of relationships and repeat any of the activities above; then use the words and phrases to practise with any Discussion Words practice activities, i.e. from *Talk a Lot Elementary Books 1-3* or *Talk a Lot Intermediate Book 1*. Or SS could use the Big Word Game or Talk a Lot Bingo from *Talk a Lot Elementary Handbook*.

7 Sentence Blocks

Note: parts of the text *in italics* will vary. SS should use their own ideas:

Brandon was playing the field with a bunch of old flames, the whole time he and Billie were an item.
(past continuous)

When was Brandon playing the field with a bunch of old flames? / The whole time he and Billie were an item. / Was Brandon playing the field with a bunch of old flames, the whole time he and Billie were an item? / Yes, he was. / Was Brandon playing the field with a bunch of old flames, *towards the end of his relationship with Billie*? / No, he wasn't. Brandon wasn't playing the field with a bunch of old flames, *towards the end of his relationship with Billie*. / So…

Who was playing the field with a bunch of old flames, the whole time he and Billie were an item? / Brandon was. / Was Brandon playing the field with a bunch of old flames, the whole time he and Billie were an item? / Yes, he was. / Was *Billie's ex-boyfriend* playing the field with a bunch of old flames, the whole time he and Billie were an item? / No, he wasn't. *Billie's ex-boyfriend* wasn't playing the field with a bunch of old flames, the whole time he and Billie were an item. / So…

Who was Brandon playing the field with, the whole time he and Billie were an item? / A bunch of old flames. / Was Brandon playing the field with a bunch of old flames, the whole time he and Billie were an item? / Yes, he was. / Was Brandon playing the field with *my cousin's sister*, the whole time he and Billie were an item? / No, he wasn't. Brandon wasn't playing the field with *your cousin's sister*, the whole time he and Billie were an item. / So…

What was Brandon doing with a bunch of old flames, the whole time he and Billie were an item? / Playing the field. / Was Brandon playing the field with a bunch of old flames, the whole time he and Billie were an item? / Yes, he was. / Was Brandon *playing chess* with a bunch of old flames, the whole time he and Billie were an item? / No, he wasn't. Brandon wasn't *playing chess* with a bunch of old flames, the whole time he and Billie were an item. / So…

What was Brandon doing, the whole time he and Billie were an item? / Playing the field with a bunch of old flames. / Was Brandon playing the field with a bunch of old flames, the whole time he and Billie were an item? / Yes, he was. / Was Brandon *being completely faithful to Billie*, the whole time they were an item? / No, he wasn't. Brandon wasn't *being completely faithful to Billie*, the whole time they were an item. / So…

How long was Brandon playing the field with a bunch of old flames? / The whole time he and Billie were an item. / Was Brandon playing the field with a bunch of old flames, the whole time he and Billie were an item? / Yes, he was. / Was Brandon playing the field with a bunch of old flames *for two weeks*? / No, he wasn't. Brandon wasn't playing the field with a bunch of old flames *for two weeks*. / So…

Extensions: Use other sentences from the dialogues (or sentences written by SS on the same topic) and practise building sentence blocks using a variety of question words and verb forms. SS can work individually, in pairs, in small groups, or as a whole class. See *Talk a Lot Elementary Handbook* for further ideas.

1 Grammar – Future Forms:

How many different future forms do you know?
Say an example sentence for each form.

Here are two common verb forms for future plans:

present continuous + time

e.g. "She's doing yoga on Thursday at 8.15 p.m."

going to + infinitive

e.g. "She's going to buy some bananas on Monday."

2 Speaking and Listening

a) Read Megan's diary for next week (right) and check any new words. Work with a partner and take it in turns to make sentences about her plans – using *present continuous* and *going to + infinitive*. You should say:

i) 10 true sentences (with positive form)
ii) 10 true sentences (with negative form)
iii) 10 false sentences (with positive or negative form)

b) Write some notes for each day to show YOUR plans for next week (or plans of a relative or a celebrity), and dictate them to your partner, who has to write them, then tell your plans back to you using full sentences and the above future verb forms. Then swap roles.

3 Pronunciation – Focus on Similar Vowel Sounds

Write 3 English words which have a stressed sound like the ones below. Dictate them in a random order to your partner, who writes them in their grid – then check and swap roles. Try to avoid saying duplicate words!

uu	oo	u	o
e.g. pudding	tattoo	lunch	borrow

Megan's Diary ♡♡!!

Monday 8.20 a.m. *dentist* (two fillings!)
After work: shopping – buy bagels, ketchup, *bananas*, potatoes, 2 packs tobacco (for Dad)

Tuesday morning: hopefully cushy *work*!
11.45 a.m. meeting with Paula – agree to project
Lunchtime: change 20 quid into Dollars
buy shampoo and *talc*

Wednesday 10.35 a.m. brunch with Ray –
deli (get him to try espresso!)
borrow memory card from Alex 512 *MB* or larger

Thursday morning: call Angie's sister –
do they still need to borrow *mattress*?
8.15 p.m. yoga at sports centre (new guru!)

Friday 7.30 p.m. whisky, *music*, guitar +
rock'n'roll = eventful evening! 10 p.m. tattoo??!!

Saturday 8.05 p.m. – meet Charlotte + Gaby
(*karaoke* – but no vodka!)

Sunday 1.15 p.m. lunch with boys at home
boomerang lesson? :)

BTW – remember pudding 4 Jo's party next Friday

My Plans: *Your Plans:*

ENGLISH IS A BIG BOILING POT OF DELICIOUS STEAMING-HOT WORD STEW!

4 Agree or Disagree? – Learning English Vocabulary

Do you agree or disagree with these statements? Say why and give examples. Find out what your partner thinks – mark ✓ for agree and ✗ for disagree:

1. I find it easy to learn new English words
2. Vocabulary is more important than grammar
3. I know more than two thousand English words
4. I try to learn at least 40 new words each week
5. I use a vocab notebook in lessons to record new words
6. I've got a good dictionary that I take with me everywhere
7. I'm interested in finding out the origins of words.
8. My first language has a large vocabulary – like English

5 Reading and Research

The English language can be compared to a big boiling pot of word stew, because it consists of words that have been borrowed over a long period of time from many different languages. It's a very open language and anybody can drop a new word or phrase into the word soup! To understand the English language is to understand a little about the history of our island race. While many of the everyday words that we use come from Anglo-Saxon words (5th Century AD), the rest come from a wide variety of sources, such as Latin, French, Spanish, Arabic, Chinese… the list is endless!

Through being conquered by other nations repeatedly, to conquering others and encouraging immigration, the English language has grown constantly for the past two and a half thousand years or so – and it's still gaining new words and expressions today! **The fact that English is not a "pure" language which developed in isolation has some important implications for students** (see bottom of page).

a) The common English words in the Diary text (left) originate from a wide range of different languages. Match the ten highlighted words with their source languages in the 4th column below (use an online etymological dictionary to help you)

b) Fill in the gaps in the 5th column by finding another example of an English word that originates from that language

Century:	Source Language:	People who Added their Languages to the Word Stew:	Example from Diary:	Another Example:
5th BC	*Celtic Languages, e.g.* Scottish, Gaelic, *and* Welsh	the original inhabitants of the British Isles	whisky	
1st BC	Latin	Roman conquerors		salary
5th AD	Old English – *a combination of three Anglo-Saxon languages*	Germanic invaders: Angles, Saxons, and Jutes		house
6th	Latin (again)	Christian missionaries from Europe led by St. Augustine	diary	
8th	Old Norse	Viking invaders from Scandinavia	want	get
11th	Old French	Norman conquerors		biscuit
15th	Middle English	Chaucer is the first writer to put into print the current mix of English, French, and Norse words	agree	scissors
13th-16th	Dutch / Flemish	traders, messengers, and explorers bring back words from Europe… (e.g. from the languages on the left)	dollar	sketch
	German		delicatessen	
	Italian		espresso	casino
	Spanish		guitar	
	Arabic	…the Middle East, and the Far East		coffee
	Sanskrit		yoga	karma
	Hindi		shampoo	
	Persian			peach
5th BC	Greek	scholars rediscover Greek during the Renaissance (15th-17th AD)		alphabet
16th	*The imagination of a genius writer from Stratford-upon-Avon*	Shakespeare is the greatest writer ever to work in English. He adds 1,700+ new words to the language	eventful	
16th-19th	*Languages from… the Americas, e.g.* Nahuatl	explorers, soldiers, missionaries, and colonisers bring new lands under English rule; as the official language of a growing Empire, English becomes a global language	potato	
	West Indies, e.g. Arawakan		tobacco	hurricane
	India, e.g. Hindi		guru	
	Africa, e.g. Fulani			jazz
	Pacific Islands, e.g. Tahitian		tattoo	taboo
	…and Australian Aboriginal languages, e.g. Wiradjuri			koala
19th	Yiddish	travellers, traders, writers, journalists, and anybody who leaves their home country, comes into contact with a new language and culture, and shares it with the folks back home…	bagel	klutz
	Chinese		ketchup	
	Japanese			judo
	Russian		vodka	pavlova
20th	*Various, e.g.* Hindi	post-World War II, citizens of former British colonies immigrate to the UK, as the British Empire disintegrates	cushy	bungalow
20th	American English	US pop culture – film, music, TV, books, etc. – introduces many new words and expressions into English	rock'n'roll	
late-20th	text-speak	English becomes the main language of computing and the internet, and is a global language once more		ur (your *or* you're)

Important implications for students:

1. We tend to keep the original spellings of the words we import, but use our native vowel and consonant sounds to pronounce them, while forcing the words to fit our stress-timed rhythm
2. Different source languages provide many synonyms in English, giving shades of meaning, and lots of options for saying the same thing
3. Unlike other languages, e.g. French, the spelling and vocabulary of English have never been formally organised and controlled
4. The fire of communication is still burning brightly, the pot is still boiling hot, and new words are being added all the time,
e.g. *The Oxford English Dictionary* recently included 400 new English words in its Twelfth Edition – words like: **woot!**, **jeggings**, and **retweet**

Can you find any more recently-added English words? Describe them to your partner and see if they can guess the meanings!

1 Grammar – Future Forms

Answers will vary, e.g. future simple with will, future continuous, future perfect, present simple for future, etc.

2 Speaking and Listening

a) Examples:

i) Megan's having brunch with Ray on Wednesday at 10.35 a.m.

ii) She isn't going to the cinema on Thursday night (because she's doing yoga at the sports centre).

iii) Megan is going to meet Charlotte and Claire on Saturday night. (false; positive form)
Megan isn't having lunch at home on Sunday. (false; negative form)

3 Pronunciation – Focus on Similar Vowel Sounds

Answers will vary. Examples of words which have these stressed vowel sounds:

uu	oo	u	o
e.g. p**u**dding	tatt**oo**	l**u**nch	b**o**rrow
w**oo**d	b**oo**t	**u**p	cl**o**ck
b**oo**k	r**u**de	b**u**t	g**o**t
p**u**t	y**ou**	l**u**ck	l**o**t
p**u**sh	p**oo**l	cl**u**b	s**o**ng
sh**ou**ld	r**ou**te	**u**nder	d**o**g
l**oo**k	d**o**	fl**oo**d	sh**o**p

5 Reading and Research

a) and b)

Century:	Source Language:	Example from Diary:	Another Example:
5th BC	Celtic Languages		Thames
1st BC	Latin	dentist	
5th AD	Old English	work	
6th	Latin		village
11th	Old French	music	
13th-16th	German		hamburger
	Spanish		mosquito
	Arabic	mattress	
	Hindi		dungarees
	Persian	talc	
5th BC	Greek	MB (megabyte)	
16th	Shakespeare		disgraceful
16th-19th	Languages from... the Americas		chocolate
	India		dinghy
	Africa	banana	
	Australian Aboriginal languages	boomerang	
19th	Chinese		tea
	Japanese	karaoke	
20th	American English		cool
late-20th	text-speak	BTW (by the way)	

(Note: the spellings of the example words in the grid on Page 2 may have changed and developed over the years; the exact dates when they first became current vary.)

Extension:

The point of this lesson is to show SS that the English words around us (e.g. in the diary extract) come from a wide variety of source languages. You could underline this by getting them to find or write a short sentence, then look up each content word in an etymological dictionary (e.g. online) to see how many different source languages they can find. It could be a competition between pairs – the winner is the student whose sentence contains words from the largest number of sources!

For example, let's examine this starting sentence from Unit 1 of *Talk a Lot Intermediate Book 1*:

The pizza restaurant will've opened by the time you get back from the beach.

The content words, which are underlined, come from four different source languages:

English Word:	Source Language:
pizza	Italian
restaurant	French
open	Old English
time	Old English
get	Old Norse
beach	Old English

Important implications for students

1. An example of this is the English word "chauffeur". The word is of French origin and in English we have kept the original French spelling from when it was first used in 1899. This word can cause a lot of problems for learners of English because of the great disparity between spelling and sound. It's not very often that "ch" is pronounced sh in English, for example. It's hard for SS to know how to deal with the vowel cluster at the end: "eur", which is transformed into a simple Schwa sound in English: uh . The English pronunciation can be spelled phonetically like this: Sheu f . Let's look at how a different language has treated the same word. The Polish language has also borrowed the word "chauffeur", instead of thinking of its own word, but has adapted the spelling to fit Polish spelling rules. In Polish the word is spelled "szofer" and it is immediately obvious for Polish speakers how it needs to be pronounced. We can see that the word originates from "chauffeur" but it has been assimilated into Polish. Why can't we do the same in English? How would a native English version of the word be spelled? Maybe "showfer", which would be much easier to pronounce on first reading than the French spelling.

The aim of any Talk a Lot course is for students to practise and improve their speaking, listening, and pronunciation skills. Along the way the student will learn plenty of new vocabulary – including non-literal English expressions, such as idioms, phrasal verbs, and slang – and also practise reading, writing, and grammar skills, e.g. verb forms, word order, parts of a sentence, and so on.

This two-page spread provides an organised sequence of learning activities for students at intermediate level (CEF B2). We believe that there is easily enough material here for a 90-minute lesson. Of course, how long the material lasts will depend on a variety of factors, such as the level of your students, and how familiar they are with Talk a Lot techniques. If you used extension activities, you could make the material last much longer.

Although many of the activities in this book can be used without having previously studied with Talk a Lot material, e.g. the reading comprehension tests, this is the second Talk a Lot Intermediate course book and the author has assumed that students will have some prior knowledge of Talk a Lot methodology, e.g. knowing how to make sentence blocks, and how to find the stressed syllables and sounds in a word or phrase; or how to read the New English Alphabet.

Describing Boring Tasks

1 Speaking Game – No Umming and Ahhing Allowed!

Work with a partner. Try to speak for twenty seconds on the topic of "describe your pen" without pausing or umming or ahhing. Keep going – try to describe every small detail, e.g. colour, shape, style, origin, use, cost, etc. Start off with ten points. For each um or pause longer than two seconds your partner deducts one point. The player with the most points at the end wins! If you can do it, increase the time! *Consider: what are good techniques for doing this?*

2 Reading

a) Read aloud the **transcript** (written version of speech) of a native speaker describing how he does a boring task – the washing-up. What do you notice about how he speaks?

"I start to run the water, hot water hopefully, put some <u>washing-up liquid</u>, not too much, just a, a little squirt, erm, pop it in, maybe run some cold water to get the lather going up. And then when it's half full **1.** I switch off the water and... but even before I switched off the water I maybe start **2.** to, erm, clean, wash the glasses, so I start off with glasses – yeah? – running the, I'm washing in the hot water with the soap, so the glasses come out really soapy and I'm <u>rinsing</u> them. I move the tap over to the left-hand side, and **3.** I'm rinsing the glass. Er, glasses . Yep? Each glass, and putting it on the top <u>drainer</u>. So there shouldn't be any <u>suds</u> on it.

"So... I start off with the hot water and the glass – all the glass stuff; then I do the cups – any cups and mugs; anything that we drink out of. That... And they're all done. And I've rinsed each one individually in the left-hand sink. Then I get into the phase, what I call, **4.** the sort of, er <u>"It's all gravy" phase</u>. So, this means it's all easy to do. **5.** I can do really quickly. I put all the plates and saucers and plates and small and dinner plates and so on, and stick them all in the water, and then this frees up space in the left-hand sink, so, er, I'm running water in the left-hand sink – just a little bit to rinse – and I'm washing the plates really quickly in the right-hand sink, and I'm washing them, erm, with the sponge, and then rinsing them in the left-hand side and sticking them on the drainer with the... with the, er, insert bits for the plates. *[Pause; clears throat]* And, er, like I said, I do this really quickly. I can do all of the plates in just, er, a couple of minutes like this.

"Anyway, er, once you've done the plates and so on, then really you've just got the bigger items to do, like **6.** the, erm, thing – the thing you use for grating cheese – saucepans, big spoons, big cutlery, and then the odd items to do. Not like the big... maybe jars and things. *[Pause]* So, I try and do the rest of it as quickly as I can, erm, all the things I've just mentioned, I put them... I drain... I sort of rinse them and then put them on the drainer. If I've got extra, **7.** then I tend to... er, put... er, I tend to put it on a, on a plastic tray by the side of... the sink, just to get dry; er, and I might even dry that up afterwards, so it doesn't look like a mess, there's still a mess there.

8. "So, erm, I've done all the... the bigger items, then I've got the <u>cutlery</u> – and I do have a special routine for cutlery as well, uh, what I... what I do there is, first of all I take all the knives out – like maybe six or seven knives, hold them in my left hand, pick them out of the left-hand sink, hold them all together and wash them in the right-hand sink, in the water, one by one, individually with the sponge – just really quickly go, take the dirt, the bits of food and grease off it, off them, then, hold them, holding them all together, I rinse them in the left-hand sink, and put them in the cutlery drainer. Then I do the same with the forks; er, then I follow the same pattern with the, with the spoons – like cereal spoons, bigger spoons. And finally just the small spoons; teaspoons – and there's usually loads of these for some reason, so I will, um, do maybe two lots of the teaspoons. And everything's rinsed; everything is nice and clean, *hopefully* – as far as I know."

b) Discourse markers such as "erm" are like verbal punctuation. They give us the chance to pause for breath before continuing our speech – without letting another person interrupt. How many of these discourse markers can you find?

c) Match the 8 features of speech below to the highlighted parts of the text:

a) Using a personal term, e.g. slang
b) Grammatical error
c) Self-correction
d) Changing a word for a more suitable synonym
e) Long rambling sentence with too many clauses
f) Grasping for what to say next
g) Using incorrect or unsatisfactory vocabulary
h) About-turn – stop and change direction

d) Where possible, find another example of each in the text.

Glossary

<u>washing-up liquid</u>: detergent that makes water soapy
<u>the "It's all gravy" phase</u>: part of the process which is easy to do
<u>suds</u>: the bubbles that are made by the detergent
<u>to rinse</u>: to run water over sth to remove the bubbles
<u>drainer</u>: the rack where plates, etc. stand to drain
<u>cutlery</u>: knives, forks, spoons, etc.

3 Reading

a) We asked the same person to **write** a description of doing the washing-up. Compare an extract from the written version with paragraph 3 of the transcript. What do you notice?

> *Then all I'm left with is the big stuff, like the saucepans and large baking trays, or awkwardly-shaped stuff, like the cheese grater and various plastic jugs. I deal with these quickly in the water, which by now is getting a bit dirty. If there is a lot of washing-up I will drain the sink and refill it with fresh water before continuing with the heavy items. I might use a metal scouring pad to clean the saucepans, depending on how encrusted with grease and bits they are…*

b) Rewrite paragraph 1 of the transcript by removing the pauses (erm, um, etc.) and correcting the errors (as in question 4). Read it aloud. What is the difference from the original version?

c) Discuss the following questions with your partner:
   i) What kind of person do you think the speaker is? What can you tell about their personality, background, age, income, education, etc. from how they speak and what they say? Give reasons.
   ii) What is *your* spoken English like? Do you leave long pauses? Do you make mistakes? Does a flood of words rush out or do you umm a lot? Do you talk in well-structured sentences? Why? / Why not?

4 Writing

Summarise how the person in the text does the washing-up into a step-by-step list of instructions using **imperative form**, for example: *1. Run the hot water…*

5 Re-order the steps for changing an ink cartridge in a printer:

____ Follow the instructions for calibrating the new ink cartridge
____ Fit the cartridge into the holder
____ Open the ink cartridge box
____ Buy a new ink cartridge which is suitable for your printer
____ Press it to make sure that it's securely in place
____ Open the front of the printer
____ Remove the outer packaging that surrounds the cartridge
____ Close the front of the printer
____ Wait for the cartridge holder to move to the right-hand side
____ Take off the plastic strip that covers the bit where the ink comes out
____ Switch on the printer
____ Take the cartridge out of the box

6 Interview

a) Your partner interviews you as you describe doing a boring everyday task, e.g. **making breakfast** or **brushing your teeth**. Record it. Try to make the steps as detailed as possible. Your partner could pretend to be an **alien**, who has no experience of this activity and needs to find out a lot of information. Here are some questions you could use:

1. How often do you do it?
2. Why do you do it?
3. Do you enjoy doing it? Why? / Why not?
4. How did you learn to do it?
5. What would happen if you didn't do it?
6. What do you think about while you're doing it?
7. Do you have a fixed routine or do you do it a different way each time?
8. Can you describe to me in detail what you do, step by step?

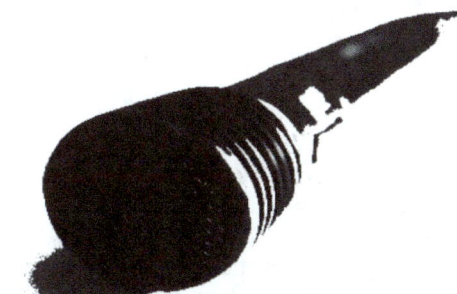

b) Change roles and repeat the activity. Then each student writes a transcription of part (or all) of their partner's audio. Study it for speech markers and features of speech as in question 4. Give your partner advice for improving their speaking skills. They then read it again, but without the pauses and errors.

7 Sentence Blocks – Imperative Form

1. First, fill the sink with hot water. [what x2, when]
2. Wash the glasses in hot soapy water. [where, what x2]
3. Next, rinse each plate in the left-hand sink. [what, where]
4. Put the forks into the cutlery drainer. [where, what]

1 Speaking Game – No Umming and Ahhing Allowed!

Extension:

A group of SS sit in a circle. One student begins talking about a boring task, but the moment they umm or pause for longer than two seconds the student on their left-hand side has to continue talking. The teacher is timing each student with a stopwatch, and the winner is the student who can continue talking for the longest!

2 Reading

b) If you count up all the pauses marked by "er", "erm", "uh", and "um" the total number is: 19. There are other discourse markers in the transcript too, where the speaker pauses for breath, or to consider what to say next, for example:

Line 1: "just a, a little squirt" – the speaker repeats a word to give himself time to think of the next phrase. This occurs again later in the transcript: "put it on a, on a plastic tray..." and once again: "with the, with the spoons..."

"so" – the speaker uses this word as a discourse marker, rather than as a conjunction with its proper meaning

"yeah?" and "yep?" – the speaker is checking that the listener is still following what he is saying

"..." this punctuation mark with three dots, called the ellipsis, is used to indicate a short pause in speech

" – " the dash is also used to indicate a short pause

[Pause; clears throat] there are a couple of times in the transcript when a pause is clearly marked. On the first of these occasions the speaker pauses to clear his throat, i.e. to cough; to clear any phlegm from his mouth so that he can speak more clearly

If we count all of the pauses in the transcript, we can say that the speaker paused 43 times in total. And perhaps there were other pauses which weren't recorded in the transcript.

c) The answer are as follows:

- a) 4.
- b) 5. (It should be: "I can do it really quickly.")
- c) 3.
- d) 2.
- e) 8.
- f) 7.
- g) 6.
- h) 1.

d) Answers will vary.

3 Reading

a) Answers will vary, but there are several key differences between the transcript and the written version. In the written version:

- there are no pauses
- there are no grammatical errors
- classic grammatical structures are used properly, e.g. first conditional: "If there is... I will..."
- the vocabulary is richer, e.g. *awkwardly-shaped* and *encrusted with grease*
- the paragraph is better ordered and follows a more logical structure
- we read what the individual wanted to present – an edited version of their thoughts – rather than a transcript of their improvised rambling speech

b) Answers will vary. Here is an example of a rewritten "tidied-up" version of paragraph 1:

"I start to run the hot water and add some washing-up liquid, but not too much. Just a little squirt. I will perhaps run some cold water to make an effective lather. When it's half full I begin washing the glasses and rinse each one under the hot water, which is still running in the left-hand sink. This is to wash off the soap, because the glasses come out really soapy. After I have finished rinsing a glass, I place it carefully onto the top drainer. There shouldn't be any suds on it..."

Extension: SS could continue rewriting more of the transcript, or all of it.

c) Answers will vary.

4 Writing

Answers will vary. Here is an example summary of the steps outlined in the transcript:

1. Run the hot water
2. Add a little washing-up liquid
3. Run some cold water to make the lather
4. Wash the glasses
5. Rinse the glasses under the tap on the left-hand side
6. Wash and rinse the cups and mugs
7. Wash and rinse the saucers and plates and put them on the drainer
8. Wash and rinse the larger items and put them on the drainer
9. If there are too many items for the drainer, put the extra ones on a tray by the side of the sink
10. Wash the cutlery, starting with the knives
11. Wash and rinse the forks, spoons, and teaspoons and put them in the cutlery drainer
12. Dry up the extra items on the tray, if there are any

5 Writing

This is the correct order:

1. Buy a new ink cartridge which is suitable for your printer
2. Open the ink cartridge box
3. Take the cartridge out of the box
4. Remove the outer packaging that surrounds the cartridge
5. Take off the plastic strip that covers the bit where the ink comes out
6. Switch on the printer
7. Open the front of the printer
8. Wait for the cartridge holder to move to the right-hand side
9. Fit the cartridge into the holder
10. Press it to make sure that it's securely in place
11. Close the front of the printer
12. Follow the instructions for calibrating the new ink cartridge

Extension: SS could put the instructions into different tenses, e.g. if you describe how you did it in the past, you could say: "I bought a new ink cartridge... I opened the ink cartridge box..." etc. Or if you want to describe how you are planning to do it in the future, you could say: "I'm going to buy a new ink cartridge..." and so on. SS could also do this for the step-by-step instructions that they create in question 6.

6 Interview

Tip: SS should try to imagine doing the activity in slow motion, so that every movement is examined and noted. For example, if you want to describe brushing your teeth, you could say: "I pick up my brush with my right hand; hold it up, then pick up a tube of toothpaste with my left hand, and open the top with my right hand. The I press the middle of the toothpaste tube so that a pea-sized amount of toothpaste comes out. I connect this toothpaste with the waiting brush head..." and so on. SS could even film themselves doing this kind of mundane activity and use the video to find out and write down exactly what they do. The aim is to analyse in detail activities that we normally do without thinking about them.

7 Sentence Blocks – Imperative Form

Note: parts of the text *in italics* will vary. SS should use their own ideas:

1. First, fill the sink with hot water. (imperative form)

What should I do first? / Fill the sink with hot water. / Should I fill the sink with hot water first? / Yes, you should. / Should I *make a cup of tea* first? / No, you shouldn't. You shouldn't *make a cup of tea* first. / So...

What should I fill with hot water? / The sink. / Should I fill the sink with hot water? / Yes, you should. / Should I fill the *bath* with hot water? / No, you shouldn't. You shouldn't fill the *bath* with hot water. / So...

When should I fill the sink with hot water? / First. / Should I fill the sink with hot water first? / Yes, you should. / Should I fill the sink with hot water *last*? / No, you shouldn't. You shouldn't fill the sink with hot water *last*. / So...

2. Wash the glasses in hot soapy water. (imperative form)

Where should I wash the glasses? / In hot soapy water. / Should I wash the glasses in hot soapy water? / Yes, you should. / Should I wash the glasses in *a cool mountain stream*? / No, you shouldn't. You shouldn't wash the glasses in *a cool mountain stream*. / So...

What should I wash the glasses in? / In hot soapy water. / Should I wash the glasses in hot soapy water? / Yes, you should. / Should I wash the glasses in *sparkling mineral water*? / No, you shouldn't. You shouldn't wash the glasses in *sparkling mineral water*. / So...

What should I do with the glasses? / Wash them in hot soapy water. / Should I wash the glasses in hot soapy water? / Yes, you should. / Should I *throw the glasses in the nearest bin*? / No, you shouldn't. You shouldn't *throw the glasses in the nearest bin*. / So...

3. Next, rinse each plate in the left-hand sink. (imperative form)

What should I do next with the plates? / Rinse each plate in the left-hand sink. / Should I rinse each plate in the left-hand sink next? / Yes, you should. / Should I *put each plate in the cupboard* next? / No, you shouldn't. You shouldn't *put each plate in the cupboard* next. / So...

Where should I rinse each plate? / In the left-hand sink. / Should I rinse each plate in the left-hand sink? / Yes, you should. / Should I rinse each plate *in the River Thames*? / No, you shouldn't. You shouldn't rinse each plate *in the River Thames*. / So...

4. Put the forks into the cutlery drainer. (imperative form)

Where should I put the forks? / Into the cutlery drainer. / Should I put the forks into the cutlery drainer? / Yes, you should. / Should I put the forks *into the fridge*? / No, you shouldn't. You shouldn't put the forks *into the fridge*. / So...

What should I put into the cutlery drainer? / The forks. / Should I put the forks into the cutlery drainer? / Yes, you should. / Should I put *the plates* into the cutlery drainer? / No, you shouldn't. You shouldn't put *the plates* into the cutlery drainer. / So...

The Hare and

1 Discussion Words

a) Translate each word from the NEA into normal spelling. Check the meaning of any that you don't know:

Fi ni shlain	_____	Ga thd	_____
hyoo Mi lii yeit	_____	Peis	_____
e Ksor std	_____	Ba j	_____
He jhog	_____	A r gnt	_____
Heir	_____	Beu sting	_____
Tor ts	_____	Dornd	_____
Kors	_____	Vi kt	_____
Pa nikt	_____		

b) Say what kind of word each is, then circle any silent letters (letters which are in the spelling, but not pronounced)

2 Focus on Punctuation Marks

a) Write the name of each punctuation mark:

, _____   ; _____   . _____

b) Match each function to a punctuation mark:

- inserts extra information
- indicates the end of a sentence
- separates items in a list
- is used before a relative clause. e.g. which, where, who, that, etc.
- separates two main clauses in a sentence, when both have a main verb
- is used before a conjunction, but not in short sentences

3 Dictation

Each student has four puzzle pieces, which are mixed up:

a) On your own: add the missing conjunctions (joining words) and relative clause words:

so (x2), and (x3), while (x2), including, as (x2), who, which

b) Add the missing capital letters and punctuation marks: , ; .

c) Dictate your texts to your partner, who writes them down. Check that the texts are correct now

d) Put the pieces in order to make the complete story

e) Find examples of each function in the complete text

f) What could be a good *alternative* title for the story? Do you have this fable (legendary story) in your culture? Is it different from this version? Tell it to your partner

47

the Tortoise

4 More Punctuation Marks

a) Name each punctuation mark, below, and write its NEA phonetic spelling:

	Normal Spelling:	NEA Spelling:		Normal Spelling:	NEA Spelling:
,	_____	_____	!	_____	_____
:	_____	_____	/	_____	_____
-	_____	_____	" "	_____	_____
—	_____	_____	?	_____	_____
( )	_____	_____	@	_____	_____

b) Mark the stressed syllable in each word or phrase. What is the stressed vowel sound in each?

c) Discuss when we need to use each punctuation mark with your partner. Get a newspaper or online text and find an example of each in use. Is it used properly? What would happen if we didn't have any punctuation marks? Are there any languages that don't?

d) What is your favourite punctuation mark? Why?

5 Listening – Track 2.4a

Listen to the mp3 file. You will hear a story read **without punctuation**. It is in eight parts, which are mixed up. The story is called *The Windmill Contest*.

Write down the text in each part, adding punctuation marks and capital letters. Change the word POTATO for a conjunction or relative clause word (as in Q.3). Compare your answers with your partner. Together put the parts into order.

6 Role Play

a) The second story is a new version of the same tale from Aesop's Fables. Find another of his fables (e.g. from **gutenberg.org**) and devise a modern version as a role play with your partner or small group. Act it out for the rest of your class. You could use, for example, *The Boy Who Cried Wolf* or *The Lion and the Mouse*.

b) Write your story, then dictate it to a new partner without giving away the punctuation (i.e. in a continuous stream of words). Your partner has to insert the punctuation marks. You could replace some of the words with a fun word, as in Q.5, above, e.g. all the articles, or all the conjunctions, are replaced by "HIPPO", and so on.

c) What do you think of stories with morals, like fables or parables? Do you like them? What function do / did they serve? What fables are popular in your culture? Why?

7 Sentence Stress & Sound Connections

i) Underline the stressed syllables and mark the sound connections (e.g. vc, cc, etc.) in these sentences from the text.
ii) Use connected speech techniques to change the sound connections into vc. Write the sentences using the NEA.

a) Whoever got the highest mark from their teacher would be the winner.

b) The teacher and all the students were astonished. and Amy's face glowed with pride.

3 Dictation – *The Hare and the Tortoise*

Student **A** – Story Puzzle Pieces.

a) Add the missing conjunctions and relative clause words: **including, and (x3), while, as, which**
b) Add the missing capital letters and punctuation marks: **,   ;   .**
c) Dictate each part to Student **B**, who writes it down; then write down what Student **B** dictates to you
d) Put the pieces in order to make the complete story

(Please cut out the four puzzle pieces below before use)

--✂--

_____ the tortoise was nowhere to be seen the hare panicked and ran the whole course as fast as he could _____ was very fast indeed _____ he reached the top of the final hill

--✂--

and steady pace _____ the hare was dancing around laughing at him other animals were laughing too _____ the rabbit the badger

--✂--

the tortoise _____ invited him to a five mile race the hare loved to race the tortoise accepted his challenge and trained hard for the event

--✂--

the tortoise was explaining patiently to the gathered friends that he had simply tried to do the best he could with the resources he had the moral is that slow _____ steady wins the race

--✂--

49

3 Dictation – *The Hare and the Tortoise*

Student **B** – Story Puzzle Pieces.

a) Add the missing conjunctions and relative clause words: **as, who, while, so (x2)**
b) Add the missing capital letters and punctuation marks: **,   ;   .**
c) Dictate each part to Student **A**, who writes it down; then write down what Student **A** dictates to you
d) Put the pieces in order to make the complete story

(Please cut out the four puzzle pieces below before use)

--✂--

_____ the hare walked around boasting that he was going to humiliate the tortoise and make him look stupid the day of the race dawned the tortoise set off at a slow

--✂--

there was once an arrogant hare _____ wanted to prove that he was better than everybody else _____ he chose the slowest animal in the county

--✂--

and even the little hedgehog the hare became exhausted from all his dancing around _____ he decided to have a nap when he awoke he realised that a few hours had passed

--✂--

he could see the finish line in the distance with the tortoise walking slowly across it the victor _____ the hare crossed the line a few minutes later red with anger

--✂--

5 Listening – Track 2.4a

Transcript:

Part 1:
POTATO amy so confident that she would win the contest hadnt even begun building yet at 10 pm she decided that she had better get started POTATO she was so tired from visiting her friends that she fell asleep

Part 2:
POTATO her rival burst into the classroom red in the face holding aloft a beautifully crafted POTATO lovingly painted toy windmill made out of brand new lolly sticks the teacher POTATO all the students were astonished POTATO amys face glowed with pride the only problem was the price tag POTATO read $25

Part 3:
POTATO she had even opened a tube of wood glue the day of the contest dawned POTATO the teacher wanted to see both windmills joan presented her model

Part 4:
POTATO a deadline of one week was set for the completion of each model joan began collecting lolly sticks straight away POTATO amy messed about visited her friends POTATO told them how she was better than joan POTATO how joans windmill would inevitably suck it was the night before the deadline

Part 5:
POTATO amy crept back to her desk joan smiled shyly POTATO explained how she had only tried to do the best she could with the resources she had the moral is that slow POTATO steady wins the race

Part 6:
POTATO was small leaned slightly to one side POTATO looked a little odd due to the fact that the lolly sticks were all dirty POTATO used joan explained that she had collected them from all around town next came amys turn her name was called POTATO she wasnt there the teacher was about to award the prize to joan

Part 7
there was once an arrogant girl called amy POTATO wanted to prove that she was the best student in the class POTATO she chose the weakest student joan POTATO challenged her to a contest both had to make a toy windmill out of lolly sticks whoever got the highest mark from their teacher would be the winner joan accepted

Part 8:
it was still visible for everybody to see dangling beneath amys model amy was humiliated POTATO joan was named the winner of the contest POTATO placed her model on the teachers desk nervously

1 Discussion Words

a) and b) Silent letters are in boxes:

NEA Spelling:	Normal Spelling:	Kind of Word:	NEA Spelling:	Normal Spelling:	Kind of Word:
Fi ni shlain	finish lin*e*	noun	Ga thd	gath*ere*d	verb
hyoo Mi lii yeit	humiliat*e*	verb	Peis	pac*e*	noun
e Ksor std	ex*h*auste*d*	adjective / verb	Ba j	ba*dg*er	noun
He jhog	he*dg*ehog	noun	A r gnt	ar*ro*ga*n*t	adjective
Heir	har*e* / hai*r*	noun	Beu sting	boasting	verb / noun
Tor ts	tort*ois*e	noun	Dornd	da*wn*ed	verb
Kors	cours*e*	noun	Vi kt	vict*or*	noun
Pa nikt	pani*ck*ed	verb			

2 Focus on Punctuation Marks

a) and b)

, comma

inserts extra information
is used before a conjunction, but not in short sentences
separates items in a list
is used before a relative clause, e.g. which, where, who, that, etc.

; semi-colon

separates two main clauses in a sentence, when both have a main verb

. full stop

indicates the end of a sentence

3 Dictation

a)-d) Here is the complete corrected text in order:

There was once an arrogant hare, **a) who** wanted to prove that he was better than everybody else, **b) so** he chose the slowest animal in the county,

the tortoise, **c) and** invited him to a five mile race; the hare loved to race. The tortoise accepted his challenge and trained hard for the event,

d) while the hare walked around boasting that he was going to humiliate the tortoise and make him look stupid. The day of the race dawned. The tortoise set off at a slow

and steady pace, **e) while** the hare was dancing around laughing at him; other animals were laughing too, **f) including** the rabbit, the badger,

and even the little hedgehog. The hare became exhausted from all his dancing around, **g) so** he decided to have a nap. When he awoke, he realised that a few hours had passed

h) and the tortoise was nowhere to be seen. The hare panicked and ran the whole course as fast as he could, **i) which** was very fast indeed. **j) As** he reached the top of the final hill,

he could see the finish line in the distance, with the tortoise walking slowly across it, the victor. **k) As** the hare crossed the line a few minutes later, red with anger, the tortoise was explaining patiently to the gathered friends that he had simply tried to do the best he could with the resources he had. The moral is that slow **l) and** steady wins the race.

e) Answers will vary. Suggested examples of punctuation use from the text:

, comma

inserts extra information:
so he chose the slowest animal in the county, the tortoise, and invited him...

is used before a conjunction, but not in short sentences
The hare became exhausted from all his dancing around, so he decided...

separates items in a list
other animals were laughing too, including the rabbit, the badger, and even the little hedgehog.

Note: some writers use a comma after the final item in a list. This is called an **Oxford comma**. Others avoid doing this. It is a matter of personal preference. I prefer to use it, as it helps to present the information more clearly.

is used before a relative clause, e.g. which, where, who, that, etc.
There was once an arrogant hare, who wanted to prove...

; semi-colon

separates two main clauses in a sentence, when both have a main verb
The tortoise set off at a slow and steady pace, while the hare was dancing around laughing at him; other animals were laughing too...

. full stop

indicates the end of a sentence
The day of the race dawned.

f) Answers will vary.

4 More Punctuation Marks

a) and b) Stressed vowel sounds are underlined:

	Normal Spelling:	NEA Spelling:		Normal Spelling:	NEA Spelling:
,	apostrophe	uh P<u>o</u> str fii	!	exclamation mark	e kskl M<u>ei</u> shn mark
:	colon	K<u>eu</u> lon	/	forward slash	F<u>or</u> wd slash
-	hyphen	H<u>ai</u> fn	" "	speech marks	Sp<u>ee</u> chmarks
—	dash	D<u>a</u>sh	?	question mark	Kw<u>e</u> schn mark
( )	brackets *or*	Br<u>a</u> kits	@	at sign *or*	<u>A</u>t sain
	parentheses	p R<u>en</u> tt seez		ampersat	<u>A</u>m p sat

c) and d) Answers will vary.

5 Listening – Track 2.4a

You can download the recording for the lesson here:

Track 2.4a: https://purlandtraining.com/tali2-track2.4a.mp3

Here is the complete corrected text in order:

Part 7
There was once an arrogant girl called Amy, **who** wanted to prove that she was the best student in the class. **So** she chose the weakest student, Joan, **and** challenged her to a contest; both had to make a toy windmill out of lolly sticks. Whoever got the highest mark from their teacher would be the winner. Joan accepted

Part 4:
and a deadline of one week was set for the completion of each model. Joan began collecting lolly sticks straight away, **but** Amy messed about, visited her friends, **and** told them how she was better than Joan, **and** how Joan's windmill would inevitably suck. It was the night before the deadline,

Part 1:
and Amy, so confident that she would win the contest, hadn't even begun building yet. At 10 pm she decided that she had better get started, **but** she was so tired from visiting her friends that she fell asleep

Part 3:
before she had even opened a tube of wood glue. The day of the contest dawned, **and** the teacher wanted to see both windmills. Joan presented her model,

Part 6:
which was small, leaned slightly to one side, **and** looked a little odd, due to the fact that the lolly sticks were all dirty **and** used. Joan explained that she had collected them from all around town. Next came Amy's turn. Her name was called, **but** she wasn't there. The teacher was about to award the prize to Joan,

Part 2:
when her rival burst into the classroom, red in the face, holding aloft a beautifully-crafted **and** lovingly-painted toy windmill made out of brand new lolly sticks. The teacher **and** all the students were astonished, **and** Amy's face glowed with pride. The only problem was the price tag, **which** read $25;

Part 8:
it was still visible for everybody to see, dangling beneath Amy's model. Amy was humiliated, **but** joan was named the winner of the contest, **and** placed her model on the teacher's desk nervously.

Part 5:
As Amy crept back to her desk, Joan smiled shyly, **and** explained how she had only tried to do the best she could with the resources she had. The moral is that slow **and** steady wins the race.

6 Role Play

a)-c) Answers will vary.

7 Sentence Stress & Sound Connections

i) Stressed syllables are underlined:

a)   Who<u>e</u>ver <u>got</u> the <u>high</u>est <u>mark</u> from their <u>teach</u>er would be the <u>win</u>ner.
         VC   CC   VC   CC   CC   CC   VC   VC   CC   VC   VC

b)   The <u>teach</u>er and <u>all</u> the <u>stu</u>dents were a<u>ston</u>ished, and Amy's <u>face</u> <u>glowed</u>
           VC   VV   CV   CC   VC   CC   VV   CV   CV   CC   CC   CC

   with <u>pride</u>.
         CC